Twayne Publishers, Inc.    ::    New York

(TUSAS) 191

# OLIVER LA FARGE

**By T. M. PEARCE**
*University of New Mexico*

For Povy La Farge Bigbee and

John Pendaries (Penny) La Farge

about Oliver La Farge has been a re-living of most of those years. La Farge first visited the Navajo Reservation in 1921, six years before I came to the University. After that our paths crossed as we met at Indian dances or when he lectured on occasions at the University. The Southwest was a vivid experience for both of us."

Thomas M. Pearce is a native-born Kentuckian, who moved in his youth to Montana, was graduated B.A., from the University of Montana in 1923; then taught at the University of Pittsburgh, where he received an M.A. in 1925 and a Ph.D. in 1930. He attended graduate summer sessions at the University of California in 1928 and the University of Chicago in 1929. "I was persuaded to add the teaching of Southwestern literature to a schedule that included Old English and Shakespeare. I agree with Oliver La Farge that American life and literature should recognize the poetry and folklore of Indian natives as English literature acknowledges the Welsh and Irish tradition before the Anglo-Saxon."

Professor Pearce taught at the University of New Mexico from 1927 to 1964, was editor of the New Mexico Quarterly from 1931 to 1939, and served as chairman of the Department of English, University of New Mexico, from 1940 to 1952. He is the editor or author of ten books, among them *Southwesterners Write, Signature of the Sun, New Mexico Place Names,* and *Mary Hunter Austin,* the last a volume in the Twayne United States Authors Series.

# Preface

A NYONE WHO SAMPLES Oliver La Farge's short stories and novels will realize that in all but two of his published volumes he sought to write about an environment alien to his own upbringing. He used his typewriter to furnish readers with twenty-two books of exotic scenes, many of them encountered in foreign fields where he worked as an ethnologist. He used his paintbrush as well as his pen to sketch the hogans of Navajos in Arizona where, as an undergraduate, he spent his summer vacations. As a boy in Rhode Island, he tried to lead the explorer's life, looking for arrowheads at early Indian campsites, hunting and fishing in the back woods as his New England forefathers had done. In later years, when he was studying anthropology in graduate school, the explorer's search led him to desert trails and jungle paths, where he sought to reestablish new points of view and to relearn the lessons of human society.

This book follows Oliver La Farge in his individual search, a quest that was never just self-centered and ingrown. He was an ingrained New Englander, but New Englanders have always been outwardgoing. There never would have been a New England without the seafaring surge of crusading founders. That impulse was compressed in La Farge, along with family pride and a native gift for writing. He loved music and would like to have achieved skill with the guitar. Disappointed in this attempt, he joined a Guitar Club in which others were the performers; he, just the listener. The club sponsored concerts; thus he became acquainted with some of the great masters of the instrument.

Since every crusader, at the outset, associates with minority groups and what are sometimes considered to be lost causes, Oliver La Farge became acquainted with relic cultures and supported them with the antiquarian's zeal. The ethical, social, and artistic values in minority ways of life were his creative and recreative hunting grounds. In his experience, they turned up in New England, the Deep South, the Southwest, and Latin America. Defending such cultures against the invasion of mass social patterns led him to assume a critical attitude throughout much of his life. His tongue was frequently barbed, and his typewriter left in print the sharpness

of his thoughts. Yet even La Farge's foes respected him for courage and conviction. His entire life was a study in pardoxes: he was a Yankee, bred to clam chowder and Boston baked beans, who acquired a taste for hominy grits and New Mexican *chile con carne*; he was a boat-lover who navigated his sailboat around the coastline of New England, yet adapted himself to cow ponies and sand twisters in the Southwest; he was an intellectual trained to date an artifact from a pottery mound, who yearned to play the guitar and to sing folk ballads.

The plan of this book falls into three parts. Part I follows a chronology which tells La Farge's story as he traveled in the East, the South, Central America, and the Southwest. He moved around a great deal, but he did settle in certain localities long enough to get an education; then he carried on field work in ethnology and published the products of this research. Part II discusses his novels and short stories as a departure from the sentimental neo-primitive tradition of fiction about the American Indian. His non-Indian fiction introduces themes and characterization new to American literature. Part III treats of La Farge, the ethnologist and historian, his theories of science and his achievement as a military historian and journalist. La Farge lectured before learned societies and museum groups, and he crusaded for a more varied and less stereotyped American culture.

I knew Oliver La Farge from the time he chose to make Santa Fe his permanent home. There he joined the group of writers who were making the city one of the creative literary centers in the United States. La Farge came to the University of New Mexico to speak in the lecture series arranged during the summer session. Since I knew him as an acquaintance, and thus not well enough to write this book without the help of many others, I am indebted to Consuelo de Baca La Farge for permission to read in her husband's study before his manuscripts were sold to the University of Texas; to Wanden Mathews Kane (the first Mrs. La Farge) and her daughter, Povy La Farge Bigbee, for interviews and for their cordial interest in this book; to Douglas S. Byers, of the Phillips Academy and the Robert P. Peabody Foundation of Archaeology, at Andover, Massachusetts. Dr. Byers was a classmate of Francis La Farge, Oliver's younger brother; and, during their senior year, both of them roomed with Oliver while he attended graduate school. Furthermore, Byers accompanied La Farge on the Navajo expedi-

tion in 1924 and on the third Tulane trip to the Guatemala high-lands. Other members of the La Farge family who have furnished me with material are Margaret La Farge Osborn and Mrs. Francis S. Childs. Mrs. Osborn wrote of the Saunderstown period and of the influence of their mother, Florence Lockwood, upon Oliver; Mrs. Childs provided biographical details in the history of the La Farge group. Alice Henderson Rossin, a long-time friend of Oliver La Farge, and an acquaintance of both Wanden Mathews and Consuelo Baca, read the manuscript and made helpful suggestions about Oliver's friendship, and Corrine Locker offered details about the Association on American Indian Affairs.

Lawrence M. Noble, Director of Admissions at Groton School, and Henry H. Richards, a retired member of the Groton staff, con-tributed information on the school days of Oliver. Henry N. Beard, librarian, and Kimbell C. Elkins, senior assistant in the University Archives, Harvard University Library, were helpful in finding source materials from the *Harvard Advocate* and the "Class Poem" from the *25th Anniversary Report*. Frances Gillmor, University of Arizona, supplied data about Apache ritual available to La Farge for *Cochise of Arizona* I am most grateful to Malcom Cowley, of Sherman, Connecticut, and to Walter L. Goodwin, Jr., another classmate of La Farge, for permission to quote from personal cor-respondence; to Margaret Mead, of the American Museum of Natu-ral History, New York City, who sent copies of her exchange of letters with Oliver La Farge written at the time both were members of the Society for Applied Anthropology; they include the "Code of Ethics" about which there was some disagreement among mem-bers of the society.

Franc J. Newcomb, of Albuquerque, permitted me to quote from a memoir describing visits of Oliver and Wanden La Farge to the Newcomb Trading Post in the early 1930's. Katherine McMahon, librarian of the Southwest Room, Main Branch, Albuquerque Public Library, and both Genevieve Porterfield and Dorothy Wonsmos, University of New Mexico Zimmerman Library, assisted in biblio-graphical documentation and the supply of source materials. In this book, as in a previous volume that I prepared for the Twayne's United States Authors Series, I am deeply grateful for the help of the editor, Sylvia E. Bowman.

T. M. Pearce

*The University of New Mexico*

# Acknowledgments

The following publishers have granted permission to quote from copyrighted compositions:

Houghton Mifflin: from *All the Young Men* (1935), *The Enemy Gods* (1937), *The Copper Pot* (1942), *War Below Zero* (1944), *Raw Material* (1945), *The Eagle in the Egg* (1949), *The Door in the Wall* (1966), *The Man with the Calabash Pipe* (1966).

*Harper's Bazaar* (April, 1935): from "No More Bohemia."

Tulane University Press: from *Tribes and Temples* (1927).

Frederick A. O. Schwartz: from La Farge's "Class Poem," printed in the "First Report of the Class of 1924."

Consuelo Baca La Farge who authorized the use of any material from her husband's published works, including "The Ancient Strength," which appeared in the *New Yorker* on August 31, 1963.

# Contents

# Chronology

1901   Oliver La Farge was born in New York City on December 19, the second son of Christopher Grant and Florence Bayard (Lockwood) La Farge. His full name was Oliver Hazard Perry La Farge, II, in honor of his noted ancestor Commodore Oliver Hazard Perry and his uncle Oliver H. P. La Farge. His boyhood was spent in New York City and at family home on Narragansett Bay, Rhode Island, where Oliver learned to ride, sail, and hunt.

1907   Student at Saint Bernard's School, New York City.

1914   Enrolled at Groton School, Lowell, Massachusetts; won letters in football, rowing, and track; also edited school magazine.

1920   Entered Harvard; rowed two years in Harvard Varsity crew; joined Circle Français, the Iroquois Club, and the Spee Social Club.

1921   Summer trip with Harvard Expedition to Tsegi Canyon, Navajo Reservation, Arizona.

1922   Joined staff of *Harvard Advocate*; wrote five stories in first year of literary activity, two of which have Navajo themes.

1923   In May 1 issue of the *Advocate*, La Farge was listed as president of board of editors; he remained president until March 1, 1924. Elected to staff of *Lampoon*. Another summer expedition to Navajo Reservation.

1924   Granted Hemenway Fellowship in Anthropology, 1924-26. Elected to Student Council. Chosen class poet. In June, received bachelor of arts degree, *cum laude*, at Harvard, with major in anthropology. In charge of expedition to Chinlee country of Arizona—his third summer among the Navajos. In autumn, enrolled in graduate school, Arts and Sciences, at Harvard; remained only the first term.

1925   Appointed assistant in ethnology, Department of Middle American Research (now Middle American Research Institute) at Tulane University, February 25, 1925—July 12, 1927; invited by Professor Frans Blom to become assistant director of First Tulane Expedition to Central America.

1926   Summer spent in Arizona; began to plan his novel *Laughing Boy*.

1927 Third Tulane Expedition to Guatemala. Publication with Frans Blom of *Tribes and Temples*. First commercial short story appeared in January issue of the *Dial*.

1928 Student again in graduate school at Harvard. Published "The Ceremonial Year at Jacaltenango."

1929 Master of arts degree from Harvard in anthropology. Returned to New Orleans for publication of *Laughing Boy*. Appointed research associate, University of Pennsylvania, from 1929 through 1931 and from 1947 until the time of his death. Married Wanden E. Mathews in New York City on September 28, 1929.

1930 Pulitzer Prize for fiction awarded for *Laughing Boy*. Winner of O. Henry Prize for short story, "Haunted Ground." Elected a director of Eastern Association of Indian Affairs; research associate, Columbia University, 1930-33.

1931 *Sparks Fly Upward*; *The Year Bearer's People*, written with Douglas S. Byers. Lecture engagements under the management of Colston Leigh, Inc., New York City. Son, Oliver Albee, born in New York City, April 30, 1931; he chose the name Pete at age eleven; died in New York City, October 27, 1965.

1932 Merger of Eastern Association of Indian Affairs with American Defense Association; La Farge became the president of the group, which later became the Association on American Indian Affairs. He served from 1932 to 1941 and from 1947 until his death. Joined Columbia University expedition to Guatemala, January to June. Honorary master of arts, Brown University, November 10.

1933 *Long Pennant*. Daughter, Povy Anya, born in New York City, August 17; now Mrs. John F. Bigbee of Encino, New Mexico.

1934 Trip to the Southwest for Association on American Indian Affairs.

1935 *All the Young Men*; also the novelette, *No More Bohemia*.

1936 Field representative for United States Office of Indian Affairs; member of secretary of interior's Advisory Committee on Arts and Sciences and also of the American Anthropological Association.

1937 *The Enemy Gods*. Divorced by Wanden E. Mathews, at Reno, Nevada, August 27; she remarried in 1940 and lives

in Fountain, Colorado (Mrs. Alexander Kane).

1939    Elected trustee of the Museum of Navajo Ceremonial Art, Santa Fe; served later as president of the board. Marriage in New York City, on October 14, to Consuelo Otille Cabeza de Baca of Santa Fe.

1940    *As Long as the Grass Shall Grow*. Oliver and Consuelo La Farge chose Santa Fe as home. La Farge resigned from League of American Writers.

1941    *The Changing Indian*, a symposium edited by La Farge. Granted a Guggenheim Fellowship; renewed in 1945.

1942    *The Copper Pot*. Commissioned as civilian historian, captain in Army Air Transport Command, September 12.

1943    Chief, Historical Division, AAF, ATC, March 2; lieutenant colonel at end of war. Awarded Legion of Honor with Commendation Ribbon military intelligence.

1944    *War Below Zero*, written with Bernt Balchen and Corey Ford (Boston).

1945    *Raw Material*, a "personal narrative."

1947    *Santa Eulalia*, from notes taken on Third Tulane Expedition.

1949    *The Eagle in the Egg* (Boston).

1950    Became columnist for Santa Fe *New Mexican*, Sunday edition, January 8.

1951    Production April 8, *The White Shell Cross*, a dance drama, written with Letitia Evans as choreographer, commissioned by Tuscon Festival of Arts. Appointed to Visiting Committee, Department of Anthropology and Peabody Museum, Harvard University. Birth of John Pendaries (Penny) La Farge on December 28 in Santa Fe.

1953    *Cochise of Arizona*. Elected a Fellow of American Association for the Advancement of Science.

1955    *The Mother Ditch*, a juvenile illustrated by Karl Larsson.

1956    *Behind the Mountains*; also A *Pictorial History of the American Indian*.

1957    A *Pause in the Desert*.

1959    *Santa Fe: The Autobiography of a Southwestern Town*, arranged with the assistance of Arthur N. Morgan.

1960    *The American Indian*, De Luxe Golden Book edition for juveniles of A *Pictorial History of the American Indian*.

1961    Controversy over the Institute of Indian Arts in Santa Fe.

1963    Taos Indian Council dispute with United States Forestry

Service over land-grant claims to Indian shrines at Blue Lake. Death of La Farge on August 2 at Bataan Memorial Hospital, Albuquerque. Funeral at Holy Faith Episcopal Church; burial in National Cemetery in Santa Fe, August 5.

1965 *Door in the Wall,* a collection of short stories ready for the printer at time of La Farge's death.

1966 *The Man with the Calabash Pipe,* selections from the La Farge column in the Santa Fe *New Mexican.*

# Part I

# THE MAN

At earliest memory, at the farthest back that I can take myself, the waters of Narragansett Bay were long familiar. The shore is always a place on which a group of boys, or one boy alone, can become utterly absorbed and self-forgetful.

My father was a great outdoors man, a wilderness man, with an unusual gift for getting on with Indians. He knew them from the Abenaki of eastern Canada to the Hopis of Arizona, and I had a secret desire to emulate him in that as well as an avowed one to emulate him in the outdoors generally.

My mother told me that in her opinion, every young man should leave his native section for a year or two and go to live in a strange place where he was unknown. In a way she was thinking along the lines of the anthropological theory that, by the study of alien cultures to which we come with fresh perceptions and without preconceptions, we shall eventually acquire a new point of view which will enable us to analyze and understand our own.

—From *Raw Material*
(Used with permission)

# Narragansett Bay, 1907-1924

O LIVER La Farge had a lively and talented group of ancestors. Indeed, if he had been given a choice, he could not have selected a more active company of forerunners on either side of his house. The French name and perhaps his artistic endowment descended from his great-grandfather, Jean-Frederic de la Farge, who joined the army of General Leclerc when Napoleon sent troops in 1801 to suppress Toussaint l'Overture in Santo Domingo. L'Overture had broken with France by conquering the eastern part of the island and by declaring it the Republic of Haiti. La Farge earned a lieutenancy in the French army; but, upon failure of the European invaders, he managed to board an English frigate for Philadelphia. He went to New Orleans, where he became a trader in the cotton market for a brief period. Among the La Farges, the story grew that he had escaped from Haiti in a rowboat and had pulled himself by oars to New Orleans. Since the distance is twelve hundred miles and since Cuba lies athwart the rower's path, the story could be called the earliest thread of romantic fiction in the La Farge tradition.

Frederic returned to Philadelphia, became an American citizen, and shortened his surname to La Farge. Assisted by connections in France, he engaged with notable success in shipping and real estate. About 1825, he moved to New York City, where he built a hotel and bought properties in Jefferson and Lewis counties along the eastern shore of Lake Ontario. This part of New York state had been settled by French immigrants who were dissatisfied with conditions following the French Revolution. In 1806, a Philadelphia company promoted new settlement; and numbers of French émigrés bought additional land. Names like Chaumont, Lorraine, Orleans, and Plessis were attached to villages in the area. At a later date, La Fargeville became one of these, taking its name from the proprietor Frederic La Farge, who built a mansion in this place for his wife Louisa Binsse de Saint-Victor. By that time, La Farge

owned a town house on Beach Street in New York City, midway between the Battery and Washington Square. Thus the La Farge family retained ties with French communities while its roots sank deep into the great metropolitan world of Manhattan Island, one of the oldest centers of American culture and the most populous as well.[1]

# I   The Grandfathers

The first of four sons born to Frederic and Louisa La Farge was John, the grandfather of Oliver. When he married Margaret Mason Perry in 1861, the La Farge family allied itself with an American family of English background with a military tradition as valorous as its own. Not long after grandfather Frederic escaped from a British fleet during his enlistment in Santo Domingo, the grandfather of Margaret Perry commanded a force which defeated a British fleet on Lake Erie. Perhaps from mutual oppositions come mutual alliances. In the New World, descendants of the British fought the British; and, in Europe, the English and French carried on feuds that had once been friendships.

Gifted traits from both lines were joined in the family of Oliver La Farge, and the given name "Oliver" was as English as the surname "La Farge" was French. "Oliver" was chosen to honor the mother's grandfather, Commodore Oliver Hazard Perry, an American naval commander during the war with Tripoli in 1811. After commanding a gunboat flotilla in New York waters, he was ordered to build the fleet for the War of 1812. In September, 1813, as Lieutenant Perry, he engaged the British warships at Put-in-Bay on Lake Erie. Following the victory, he sent to General Harrison the now famous message: "We have met the enemy and they are ours." Six years after this achievement, he died of yellow fever while serving on a government mission to Venezuela. He was only thirty-four years old. Was it chance or a more guided fortune that Oliver, a descendant about his age, should follow his path to Latin America and pursue studies among the same Indians around the Caribbean shore?

John La Farge built a summer home for his family in Newport, Rhode Island. The family lived in various rented houses in the changing New York City of that day, but John kept the same studio at 51 West Tenth Street within easy reach of Washington Square, the center of New York's literary and artistic activities.[2] When John was twenty-one years of age, he sailed to Europe to visit the gal-

leries of art and the monuments of architecture. The brilliant murals and gleaming windows in great buildings awakened in him the desire to create wonders of their kind in his own land. He studied long enough and traveled widely enough to choose art as a career.

Upon returning to the United States, John La Farge discovered how little had been done with mural decoration. The pioneer in the field was his teacher William Morris Hunt, who had a studio on Church Street in Newport.[3] Encouraged by this mentor, La Farge designed a mural for the new Episcopal Church of the Ascension in New York City. The painting dramatized the risen Christ with angelic choirs singing beside Him as He extended a hand in blessing above the disciples grouped below. Art critics praised the symmetry of the separate groups and the harmonies of color, acclaiming the work as the greatest mural which had been produced in America.

All about him in New York, John La Farge watched the building not only of great churches but of great domestic mansions, even of palaces on such thoroughfares as Fifth and Madison avenues. One of these was the Romanesque chateau called Tiffany House, which Charles Lewis Tiffany built to display his treasures in painting, textiles, jewelry, iridescent glass, and ceramics. Tiffany's son, Louis Comfort, invented the famous glass which spread a rainbow play of colors over lampshades, vases, and windows throughout America. All through John La Farge's period, he also experimented with a new process for making stained glass. He used the process for making church windows, which may have led to the environment in which his son Christopher Grant, Oliver's father, developed an interest in ecclesiastical architecture. At least Grandfather John could claim some influence in the background when his son Grant in 1890 submitted the winning design for the Cathedral of Saint John the Divine in New York City. The architectural firm, Heins and La Farge, was engaged to draw plans and to supervise construction of the third largest edifice for worship in the world.

## II   *The Father*

Christopher Grant La Farge was born in Newport, Rhode Island, on January 5, 1862. The John La Farge home at Sunnyside Place was only a ten-minute walk from Narragansett Bay. Close by were summer homes of many prominent Bostonians, New Yorkers, and other visitors from places as distant as the Deep South. Before her marriage, grandmother Margaret La Farge had met Louisiana

sojourners at Newport and had accepted an invitation to visit their plantation. One of the shaping influences in Oliver La Farge's life was the creative period when, as a young man, he lived in New Orleans not far from the places his grandmother had visited and his great-grandfather had lived as a refugee.

Across the bay from Newport in Saunderstown was the home of Florence Lockwood, who was to marry Grant La Farge in 1895. The Lockwood house was a treasure from colonial days, with fine workmanship in door frames, porch columns, moldings, and pediments. When Grant enrolled at the Massachusetts Institute of Technology, he decided to study architecture. His earliest professional designs were drawn for homes and business structures. Then, when the firm of Heins and La Farge was organized in 1886, he devoted his time chiefly to church buildings. The style in which the Cathedral of Saint John was drawn was Romanesque, a design suggested to Grant La Farge by the great church of Gerona, which he had seen on his visit to Spain as a young man. When the firm of Heins and La Farge was replaced seven years later by the partnership of Cram and Fergusson, Oliver was eleven years old.

The entire family felt the disappointment of Grant La Farge after his firm lost the contract for constructing the cathedral. The Spanish Romanesque style was replaced by French Gothic. Was loyalty to the Spanish tradition in his father's design an influence upon Oliver to respond with warmth to the Spanish tradition in Central America and the southwestern United States?[4] George Heins died in 1907, but the firm continued under the name La Farge until it became La Farge and Son in 1931. After the bank failures and the depression of 1929, Grant La Farge's strength failed. He retired to the Saunderstown home where he had spent so much of his leisure time while his daughter and three sons were growing to maturity.

## III   *The Mother*

Florence Bayard Lockwood, the mother of Oliver La Farge, was of French descent in one branch of her family. The Bayards were Huguenots, as Protestant as the La Farges were Roman Catholic. Prominent in the American political scene, they included in their number five United States senators, a secretary of state, and an ambassador to the Court of Saint James. The Lockwoods, too, were Protestant; but not much is known of grandfather Benoni Lockwood, who sailed a clipper ship and fought the Tripoli pirates

after President Jefferson asked Congress to declare war against them. Florence Lockwood was Episcopalian, and her children were instructed in accord with their mother's religious convictions. Details of grandfather Lockwood's life may have been incorporated, imaginatively, into Oliver La Farge's novel *Long Pennant*, although the pirates were transported from the Mediterranean to the Caribbean.

A number of the Lockwood families were neighbors of the La Farges in Saunderstown. "There was a whole tribe of us," writes Oliver's sister, Margaret La Farge Osborn. "We did everything together, games, boating, swimming, much conversation with the grownups, including a great intellectual game called 'Twenty Questions,' which sometimes lasted for days with many trips to the *Encyclopedia*. All in all we had a most wonderful youth. One of the things I remember best is Oliver sitting on the floor of the living room in an Indian costume that came from Schwartz Toy Store and very solemnly smoking a peace pipe. My father called him 'Indian man.' I suppose he was between eight and ten when he got the costume."[5]

Mrs. Osborn recalls that her mother was something of a scholar and took a great interest in civic affairs: "I think some of Oliver's later interest in helping the Indians came from that. We always heard so much from her about doing our share in things, and she had a really remarkable gift with people in the house, from ambassadors to furnace man. One never knew who would be there for tea time with her." When Theodore Roosevelt, his wife, and his son came to visit, Roosevelt gave Mrs. La Farge cuttings from Mount Vernon to start a box hedge for her garden. Owen Wister, a close friend of the La Farges, lived about three miles away and was often a visitor in their home. Both Wister and Roosevelt were easterners with an enthusiasm for the American West. Wister, a Philadelphian, made his first trip to the West in 1885, the year he entered Harvard Law School; and he repeated his visits before and after publishing *The Virginian* in 1902. Wister knew Roosevelt in the 1890's, after Roosevelt had purchased a South Dakota ranch and acquired the picturesque western mannerisms which became associated with his personality. Roosevelt's platform manner and his spoken and written style were marked by the ease and casual manner of the West.

Certain aspects of a child's endowment may be traced to one or the other of his parents. Grant La Farge made Oliver at home in

the out-of-doors, helping him to adapt to nature as a woodsman, hunter, fisherman—all a background for his life as an anthropologist. Florence Lockwood La Farge deepened his social insights, through the variety of her contacts and her probing inquiries into the problems of groups and communities. Both parents were cultivated in their tastes for art and music. In addition, they were vigorous and creative in their points of view.

## IV  *Saint Bernard's School*

Books were everywhere in the Saunderstown house, not only in bookcases, but on every table. "We had the habit of reading," writes Oliver La Farge, "and weren't afraid of studying matters supposed to be beyond our years."[6] This statement may explain the "head start" the La Farge children had when they went to school and also the independence at least one of them showed when he had to follow rules and regulations in those schools selected for him to attend. Saint Bernard's School at 4 East Ninety-eighth Street in New York City enrolled pupils only in the primary grades. Oliver has nothing but praise for his years at Saint Bernard's, where he showed none of the resentment which he registered later for his preparatory school in Connecticut. Perhaps the fact that the classrooms were closer to home and that he did not live-in at Saint Bernard's had something to do with the amiable response the school brought forth. He found the students and the staff to be congenial. The classroom hours in both science and literature were stimulating. Horizons of mythology were opened by great stories like the *Iliad* and the *Odyssey*. Heroes of the past, from Achilles and Hector to King Arthur and Charlemagne, not only lived as fiction but also provoked the curiosity which led Oliver to the study of archaeology, anthropology, and the beginnings of the arts in human development.

## V  *Groton School*

From Saint Bernard's, where the classrooms were located above the clatter of city streets, Oliver carried his studious attitudes and nervous physical energies to Groton School, situated on the Nashua River west of the industrial town of Lowell, Massachusetts. This school was established near a farming district in 1793 and was named for the village where it is located. At first it was an academy for children of both sexes, but later it became an exclusive preparatory school only for boys. Scholastic standards were high, following

the patterns of such English schools as Eton and Harrow. Groton aimed to draw a superior class of students to its academic precincts, and it succeeded.

Oliver never complained about the academic program, but he experienced almost total maladjustment in the social community. Life at home, according to La Farge, had been "in many ways a child's heaven, a happy, roaring democracy with a touch of anarchy, ruled by reason and justice tempered with indulgence. We were allowed to argue about anything that came up and argue we did, particularly at table, be it over the depth of the channel in Narragansett Bay or what was the matter with the Darwinian theory. We were always getting up from the table to find a reference book."[7] He concedes that his father just tolerated this turmoil but that his mother found it stimulating. Acting as umpire in every dispute, she suppressed temper tantrums and encouraged the use of logic in searching for answers.

Headmasters at Groton were doubtless not enthusiastic about a "roaring democracy" on the campus. They had their own methods of inculcating knowledge; and, in addition, they had the housing, feeding, and disciplining of several hundred young men, some of whom did not adapt easily to what La Farge calls Groton's "totalitarian community." One of Oliver's schoolmates writes: "La Farge was an individualist even at those times and, I might add, in an atmosphere where it was most certainly discouraged by both faculty and boys. They certainly made it hard sledding for those who were at all different and La Farge didn't give in to the pressures in any way, beyond the bare necessity of staying there."[8]

Instead of following the regulations, La Farge resisted them as much as he could and tried to cut a path for himself as in later years he used a machete to make a path through tropical underbrush in Mexico and Central America. He admits that the battle was largely within himself; he wanted to win attention and to achieve distinction, and he had not yet found how. To a lesser degree, he wanted to be a part of the activities in sports. He discovered that he could high jump, and he earned a place on the football squad; but he was too light to pursue this career in a contact sport. Besides this handicap, the coach disgusted him with his vulgar language and overemphasis upon winning at all costs.

But Oliver was not really a wholehearted athlete: baseball bored him, and his temperament unsuited him for perfection in high

jumping. The long pauses between action were boring. The sports he really enjoyed were those of his boyhood at home—fishing, hunting, and boating; they were related to his life, not just to entertainment or physical achievement. The comments La Farge makes about school-day sports are those of a man preparing to write about, as well as take part in, action. He knew at an early age that he wanted to be a writer. His name "Inky" is a symbolic tab showing that he held a pen at the earliest possible moment.

When Oliver was in the fourth form at the age of fifteen years, his mother sent him a review of a book by Henry Fairfield Osborn. The review was written by Theodore Roosevelt, and the title of the book was *Men of the Old Stone Age*. Both the text and the drawings in the volume made use of data about human bones and artifacts recently found in caves located all the way from the Pyrenees Mountains to sites in Austria and the Rhine country. Polychrome frescoes of bison, reindeer, and wild boars, which had been painted by Cro-Magnon artists twenty-five thousand years before the Christian era, led these anthropologists to reassess the cultural stages of primitive mankind. Osborn wrote with a romantic touch about the sometimes prosaic task of excavating archaeological layers to uncover the life of early eras. He was of the European school in his teaching and research; his inquiries were devoted to the anthropology of the Old World. He does, however, refer to the Late Stone Age in the fourth glacial period as being contemporaneous in Europe and North America. Later anthropologists were to tell how Asiatic animals found a way across the land bridge of the Bering Strait area into Alaska and how human beings following the giant bison, musk-ox, and woolly mammoth into North America, living off their flesh and using their skins for shelter and protection.[9] Oliver La Farge at high school age was reading about the evidence for early man and perhaps shaping vague plans to investigate this field of research. Not many years were to pass before this investigation became possible for him.

## VI  *Harvard Days*

The link between Groton and Harvard was not entirely intellectual for La Farge. Many of the Groton alumni went to Harvard, and a number of his teachers at the preparatory school were Harvard men; but the tie-in between higher and lower education for Oliver at this time was rowing. He had acquired a love for rowing during

his fifth form at Groton, one of the few preparatory schools which had crews. During this year he first sat in a machine where he learned the swing of the oars, the push of knees and feet, the rhythm of shoulders, back, and hips. He won a letter in this sport, and his passion for the eight-oared shell became a dynamic, singing, poetic thing which he described in one of the most eloquent prose descriptions of an American sport.[10]

Other activities at Harvard, such as editorial work on the *Advocate*, may have contributed more to his professional career; but nothing gave such a lift to his spirits, or such justifiable pride, as his place with seven other oarsmen, each of whom was balancing a twelve-foot oar in a narrow shell and then pulling to drive the craft through the water. "Rowing is set in beauty," he wrote, as he described the open country around a rural stream or the wide basin for water sports: the sunlight, cloud shadows, grassy slopes, bridges, walls, factory signs—a panorama of forms and outlines sliding past the racing prow! The crash of oars in locks, the roll of seats forward and back, the strain of muscles—all became synchronized into a continuous forward thrust until the goal was reached. Then tired bodies slumped over oars; the boat slowed to a stop. During the race, eight men were pulling as one; the coxwain's voice spoke for all; his will became theirs. Win or lose, the men merged identities for a brief time and became a part of one another.

From La Farge's report, the coxwain of his crew was as profane as his football coach had been. Either the personalities of the two men were so dissimilar as to cause one to be appealing and the other the reverse, or the sports were so different as to condone vulgarity in one and condemn it in the other. Whatever the cause, words from a "foul-mouthed, brilliant little devil" in an eight-oared shell inspired La Farge, whereas the "ugly snarling" of a pigskin mentor had depressed him. When Oliver rowed bow in the first 150-pound shell at Harvard in 1923, one of his crew mates gave the following description of his appearance: "He often stepped onto the float with a look of utter ecstasy on his face after one of those days when the very shell itself seemed a vibrant living thing, pulsing with life at each catch and pull."[11]

At Harvard University, Oliver La Farge no longer felt the insecurity of his previous school years; the daydreams and the impulses of withdrawal disappeared. He plunged into activities as

though they were an end in themselves, joining several clubs and applying for membership on the staff of the *Harvard Advocate*, the oldest of the literary journals, having been founded in May, 1866. It appeared fortnightly and contained fiction, poetry, essays, and editorial comment.[12] Oliver served his apprenticeship on the magazine and became a member of the editorial board in 1922. In this year he also became a member of the Harvard Student Council and was chosen for the staff of the humor magazine, the *Lampoon*. He admits that he sought this post for prestige and that he was not congenial with the staff members nor they with him.[13] Humor of a broad sort was not one of the gifts possessed by Oliver La Farge.

Literary work on the *Advocate*, however, was his introduction to professional writing. From the publication of his first story in the issue of October 1, 1922, to his last story on June 1, 1924, La Farge wrote thirty-four separate pieces for the magazine. Eight of these contributions were short stories; nineteen, nonfiction; seven, poems. The nonfiction consisted of ten editorials and nine essays. As La Farge's career unfolded in later life, only the poetry fell by the wayside. A new type of writing was added, the scientific article, which he sometimes expanded to book length.

The titles and plots La Farge chose for stories in the *Advocate* indicate how a young writer explores his mind in search of landscapes and characters to put on paper. The first story, which deals with the sea, is "Captain Tom and Mother Carey's Chickens." The location is Narragansett Bay, and the narrator is an old tar in the forecastle of a two-master at anchor during stormy weather. The sailor regales his listeners with a fanciful account how the sea birds avenged the death of one of their mates. While the lamp swings in great circles, casting irregular shadows on the bunks and ceiling, he tells of Captain Tom Pearse, one of the king's men, whose job it was to capture rum runners. On a day when Captain Tom was in a particularly bad humor, he killed a petrel, one of "Mother Carey's chickens." In punishment, Mother Carey sent a raging storm and also created a breakwater to shut Captain Tom's boat from the bay. Trying to return, the Captain saw anchor lights like the false lights he used to hang out to cause shipwrecks. He turned his boat around and steered for the lights. When the rocks confronted him, he sailed over them, cursing the wind and the shoal water until his ship disappeared in the darkness on the land.[14] The story is a combination

of fancy and realism. La Farge merges the memories of storms and sailing boats with the lore of birds and the forces of nature, weaving a background of mystical punishment upon Captain Pearse, the king's man.

Some four months later, in the fifth number of the magazine, he published another story, "The Two Grenadiers." The setting is in southern France, and the reader listens as two of Napoleon's soldiers discuss the emperor's escape from Elba. They are weary from their past military campaigns, but they drink a salute to their general as new troops march to join him.[15] The sixth number of the *Advocate* containing a La Farge story appeared in his third year at Harvard, 1922-23. He wrote about a canyon called "Batata-kin," a strange name from what seemed to be a foreign tongue. Yet the word is American Indian and it identifies a cliff which Oliver had visited during the previous summer in Arizona. This had been an archaeological field trip arranged by Professor Alfred Tozzer. The story concerns a young Navajo named George Owl, who has returned to his people after four years of college. He brings a bachelor of arts degree in civil engineering and is also an amateur anthropologist. An old medicine man urges him to spend the night in the canyon where the ancestors or "Ancient Ones" had lived. Dressed in a buckskin shirt, breechclout, and moccasins, George Owl rides to the ancient ruins where he builds a fire, smokes a cigarette, and sleeps for a time near the glowing embers. When he awakens, he hears a wolf call and finds that the fire is out. Above him are the outlines of old houses. He starts to climb the canyon wall. Something moves in the doorway of a ruined dwelling where a fire seems to glow inside the house. Other spots show in dark places, and howls come from all around him. He answers with a wolfish shriek of his own and shoots arrows at the glowing spots until the last arrow is gone. Suddenly, something strikes his head. A blaze of fire is followed by pain and darkness. The next morning the Navajos find him dead, still clinging to his war-bow and long knife.[16]

These stories indicate the varied fields for writing which were open to La Farge, those which were close to New England and its associations and those which were opening to him as he traveled and studied ethnology. He chose for a time to make use of new experience, but he later drew upon his life in New England. As he writes, he makes constant reappraisal of himself. The search becomes one for identity, a seeking to find the most permanent self

among many selves. While La Farge was secretary to the Board of the *Advocate* and later president, someone on the staff wrote a number of editorials entitled "The Man with a Briar." The narrativelike sketches are amusing accounts of the narrator in conversations with others who may be real or imaginary. This same framework was chosen by La Farge twenty-six years later when he became a columnist for a newspaper in Santa Fe, New Mexico, then his home. The only difference is that the Santa Fe writer calls himself "The Man with the Calabash Pipe" instead of "The Man with the Briar."[17]

The choice of anthropology as a major at Harvard may have been influenced by Oliver's father. In 1922, Grant La Farge drew the illustrations for *American Indian Life*, a volume edited by Elsie Clews Parsons, who had been writing about the ceremonial and clan life of the Pueblo Indians. In the following year, she published a collection of Navajo folk tales.[18] Both of these Indian groups drew the interest of the younger as well as the older La Farge. In June, 1924, Oliver was graduated with a bachelor of arts degree *cum laude* and at the commencement exercise read the poem he had written after being elected Class Poet. Called "Baccalaureate Hymn," it embodies his deep sense of obligation to fulfill a commitment within himself to God and to his country. The lines state that no man's life is without a purpose. The first stanza of the poem describes a ship going out into the world, seizing the wind and bearing the flag to distant lands, then returning with spices and furs. Following this outburst of enthusiasm, the graduating poet expresses a note of cynicism, contradicting the romance of the voyager:

> And so it goes, the ancient balderdash,
> And adolescent burst of hopefulness,
> While aged seamen, o'er their sour beer,
> Foretell how soon we'll learn to reef our sails
> And trim them to convenience, tell in short
> How soon we'll be like them, how soon deny
> Vigour and daring and all foolishness.
> Oh we'll soon learn!

The stanza which continues this pessimism contends that most of the class will never attain more than mediocrity and will exist like the rest of society, plodding along in a pattern fixed by their neighbors in politics, religion, and profession. They should, there-

fore, praise the college hours when they were offered a glimpse of the heroic action of great men and their search for truth. The poem concludes:

> Yea, now we raise our voices up on high
> Gladly, and mark upon our memories,
> However may our spirit in the years
> Flicker and fail, and our keen blades grow dull,
> Here for a while, in very truth, we lived.[19]

## VII   *Third View of the Navajo Country*

The final trip of the Harvard Navajo Expeditions was under Oliver La Farge's leadership. This was in the summer of 1924. On the first and second trips in 1922 and 1923, he had been an undergraduate. Now he was in complete charge of a field exploration and responsible for its success or failure. One of the research members of this project was Douglas S. Byers, then in his senior year at Harvard. Today, as director of the Peabody Foundation of Archaeology at Andover, Byers is recognized as an authority on the Navajos and their ethnology. He recalls excavating ruins on the 1924 trip at Nokaito near Chinlee, a trading post five miles from an Arizona state highway and about thirty-five miles from Fort Defiance and a government Indian school.

When the expedition disbanded at the end of summer, La Farge and two others decided to ride to the Grand Canyon. The distance was one hundred and forty miles; they bought horses from the camp wrangler and started out. Crossing a landlocked island called Black Mesa, they stopped to spend the night within sight of one of the round houses in which Navajos live. Several Indians rode over to invite them to supper. Navajo meals usually consist of boiled beef or mutton stew with potatoes and other vegetables, such as beans, fried squash, or pumpkin. As the Anglo-Americans left, they invited the Navajos to breakfast the next morning. When the Indians came, La Farge served them boiled rice sweetened with dried peaches that had been soaked and simmered during the night. Brown sugar and evaporated milk added the touch of flavoring, and hot coffee washed the ingredients down. The night before he had exchanged stories and learned to recognize Navajo jokes when he heard them.[20]

That autumn La Farge returned to graduate school at Harvard; but, after the first term, he heard from Professor Tozzer, his patron

and adviser, that Professor Frans Blom of Tulane University was organizing an expedition to proceed from Mexico City to Guatemala to investigate the sites of ancient Mayan ruins. Since Oliver's Hemenway Fellowship had been extended, he was free to join the Tulane group. With the background of field work obtained in Arizona, he felt competent to associate with scientists who were experienced in research techniques. Anthropology had brought him into the laboratory of primitive life where he could observe and record without the help of textbooks written by others. In such research he could find the origin of politics, religion, art, and storytelling.

From the outset of this post-college period there were two La Farges: one, the scholar, aware that scientific journals would publish his investigations; the other, the artist, observing the color and drama in tribal ways. The two were locked in a struggle for mastery. Although the scientist won at the start, the triumph was short-lived. The artist sprang to the fore, until the combat was renewed and neither the imaginative man nor the scientific investigator was ever entirely free of the other. As his life unrolled, Oliver La Farge functioned effectively in both scientific and creative fields.

# New Orleans, 1925-1929

W HETHER LA FARGE ever looked forward to teaching as a profession is not clearly indicated. A character in one of his novels remarks, "Teaching was a job all right, a chore, a bore."[1] Although he signed a contract as an assistant in ethnology at Tulane University, he may have known when he signed it that members in that department did not then teach classes. At one place in his memoirs he refers to the drudgery of obtaining a doctorate.[2] He may have found academic life agreeable, but the assistant or research worker had to climb the academic ladder; the climb was tedious and not always rewarding. It is doubtful that La Farge would have shown the patience for such a process; he was in a hurry.

La Farge's information was prodigious in many fields. His platform manner was effective, and he spoke fluently both in private conversation and before public assemblies. Furthermore, he looked like a professor, with his erect, slender figure, his sharp, intellectual features, his dark-rimmed glasses, his serious, straightforward glance. Fortunately, he never had to make the choice between teaching and commercial writing. Success came to him in a big way with the publication of his first novel in 1929. Yet, before this favorable development, three years elapsed during which he was carrying on research in anthropology, research that took him into the amphitheater of native American life south of the United States and into the great centers of pre-European sculpture, hieroglyphs, and architecture in Central America.

## I  *First Expedition to Central America*

La Farge's destination when he left Harvard Graduate School in 1925 at mid-year was New Orleans, where Tulane University had just established a Department of Middle American Research. Hans Blom had been employed to organize the first field trip. Blom was born in Denmark in 1893 and was, therefore, eight years older than La Farge. Having earned his Bachelor of Philosophy at the Univer-

sity of Copenhagen, he went on to add the Master of Arts at Harvard in 1925. After the trip with La Farge in 1925, Blom became director of the Middle American Research Institute (as it was renamed) and continued in the directorship until 1941. He lived the remaining twenty years of his life in Chiapas, the Mexican state he had explored during his first year at Tulane.

Professor Blom left New Orleans on February 9, just as the city was cheering the Mardi Gras parade. He traveled by boat to Tampico, Mexico, taking with him the greater part of the equipment needed for the expedition. Oliver arrived in New Orleans before Hans left and waited there a few days; then he traveled by land to Mexico City. Blom was there so that they could arrange for government permits, letters of introduction, and other official documents needed for the trip. Blom was Archaeologist in Charge; Oliver, Ethnologist and Assistant. They were the entire staff except for the guides they hired in communities where Mayan antiquities were to be inspected.

One of these guides, Lazaro Hernandez Guillermo, whom they found in San Fernando, Chiapas, remained with them throughout the trip. He became so necessary to its success that, when the book *Tribes and Temples* was written, he was listed as Guide and as a member of the staff. Blom reports that Guillermo acquired the nickname Tata, which meant something like father in the speech of the Chiapas Indians. The word was a mark of respect to older men.[3] Guillermo's virtues were notable in the attention he paid to the four mules that made up the pack trains. He called them his *niños* and never rested at night until the animals were washed down, fed, and made comfortable. He never once swore at them or struck one in anger. He treated the horses with the same care and respect. The Americans found, however, that the *ladinos*, or mestizos, did not regard the Indians with the courtesy due equals. They resented serving Tata and sitting down with him when the staff was served food at their tables. The American scientists, who worked with Guillermo all day, continued to eat with him at meals.

The First Tulane Expedition to Middle America ended in August, six months after the equipment had been loaded on the steamer at New Orleans. The pack train had proceeded from the Gulf town of Frontera, through the states of Tabasco and Chiapas and into Guatemala. A few days before the Americans left Mexico, they climbed an almost vertical street in a small village, and Oliver's

horse tumbled over backward and fell on him. For a few moments, the accident appeared to be serious, but, when horse and rider were separated, neither had broken anything. They were bruised but able to travel. The expedition was not delayed.

In the following month, La Farge again signed his contract at Tulane. He gave time to writing his reports and to helping with the text of *Tribes and Temples*, which was being published by the Tulane University Press. The numerous photographs, maps, and drawings make the book of interest to the general reader as well as to the scientist.

## II    *The Third Tulane Expedition*

Summers were usually free for research assistants to continue their graduate study, either at an institution where they were working or elsewhere. Oliver had been so successful in the first journey of exploration that Blom placed him in charge of the Third Expedition, organized in 1927. The prefatory letter which Blom affixed to *The Year Bearer's People* when it was published in 1931 is addressed to the president of Tulane and explains that the purpose of this third trip had been decided when he and La Farge were in Chiapas in 1925. They had learned that Indians in Guatemala still observed a ceremony honoring a person called "the Year Bearer." The extant Mayan codices and the oldest Spanish manuscripts reported such a ritual in which four days related to the equinoctial periods should be set apart to begin a new year. It was to learn more about the Year Bearers that La Farge started south again.

This expedition lasted from February through April. He was fortunate to have with him Douglas Byers as the assisting scientist, for they had been coworkers during the Arizona summer three years earlier. The third member of the staff was Jose María Hernandez, a *ladino* of Jacaltenango, who was well educated and a scientist at heart. He was familiar with native customs and spoke Spanish, English, Jacalteca, and some French. La Farge wrote most of *The Year Bearer's People*, but the field notebooks are credited equally to Byers and La Farge.

## III    *New Orleans: Cultural Adaptation*

In New Orleans, Oliver lived on Saint Peter's Street at the north-

west side of the French Quarter. His apartment was more than three miles from Tulane University, the campus of which spread north from Audubon Park and touched the edge of the Mississippi River. He must have chosen this location near Beauregard Square because the area was picturesque and yet not as lively as the heart of the Vieux Carré proper, where tourists and patrons thronged the shops and bars. Beauregard Square was once the site of old forts on Rampart Street. Later the area was a circus ground, and it finally became a park enclosed by an iron fence and ornamented with an equestrian statue of General P. G. T. Beauregard, who had led the Confederates at Fort Sumter, Bull Run, Shiloh and other Civil War battlefields.

La Farge, at this time, lived somewhere between the scholar's study and the artist's studio. He was vacillating between the career of a linguist collecting dialect forms among Indians and that of the writer scribbling a novel, probably one about the people who were speaking the very dialects he had been studying. He began to write the novel, but he also began to face the problems caused by giving up a professional life already under contract.

In post-Civil War days, New Orleans had nourished the literary gifts of George Washington Cable, Lafcadio Hearn, Grace King, Ruth McEnery Stuart, and others who drew upon the folklore surrounding the old streets and gardens of the city. Before the Civil War, the writers using French had written romantic tales of Indian and Creole life in Louisiana settings. Walt Whitman worked on a newspaper in New Orleans, and Samuel Clemens acquired his pen name following his steamboat days between Saint Louis and the great port at the mouth of the Mississippi Delta. William Sidney Porter (O. Henry) is said to have taken refuge in New Orleans when he first fled from Texas to escape charges of embezzlement; and, while in the city, Eugene Field was haunting the antique shops and writing poems about voodoo doctors whom he encountered. When La Farge lived, as he says, "in the Quarter," Sherwood Anderson was writing *Dark Laughter* there; and such writers as William Faulkner, Ernest Hemingway, Thornton Wilder, Roark Bradford, and Carl Carmer were either in residence or of recent memory.

As a kind of confession, Oliver states that New Orleans taught him to enjoy life and not to feel responsible for all of life's trials and tribulations. While he was in the South, he tried to acquire some of the warmth he noticed in the courtesy around him. He had decided

that the compliments exchanged in social relationships were not necessarily insincere. Because some of his own attitudes led girls to think him unpolished and crude, he practiced the little pleasantries he heard in southern discourse; but his New England restraint yielded slowly to more relaxed attitudes.

La Farge then analyzed himself in terms of his own ethnological formulas: he was experiencing cultural adaptation and substituting one set of preferences for another. As a Yankee among southerners, he found values to accept and to reject. One thing he knew was happening: the scientist was evolving into the writer. His French Quarter apartment on Saint Peter's Street was known as "The Wigwam" and was becoming a gathering place for artists and writers, including some scientists as well.[4] Decisions of far-reaching importance for Oliver La Farge were imminent.

## IV  *The Origin of* Laughing Boy

During the time La Farge was organizing his notebooks on linguistics and ethnology, he was planning a novel about the Navajo Indians. He arranged to go on halftime schedule at Tulane in order to have the mornings free to write. Some years after he left Louisiana, he gave an interview to a reporter for the *Providence Bulletin* of Rhode Island. In answer to a question, he said that the idea for his novel *Laughing Boy* came to him two and a half years before the book was published.[5] Since the novel was published in 1929, this pinpoints the date for its inception as the time La Farge returned to the Navajo Reservation in the summer of 1926. He had written a story using a Navajo theme, "North Is Black." The story was purchased by *Dial* magazine and was published in January, 1927.

In this issue were also stories, articles, and poems by such well-known writers as Benedetto Croce, William Carlos Williams, Yvor Winters, Sacheverell Sitwell, Witter Bynner, and Gilbert Seldes. In the same volume, other figures of note are represented, among them Conrad Aiken, Kenneth Burke, Padraic Colum, T. S. Eliot, D. H. Lawrence, Thomas Mann, and Marianne Moore. *Dial*, edited by Miss Moore from 1926 to 1929, was associated with the new creative movements in the early decades of the twentieth century. To make a bow on the literary stage in such company was a great achievement for a twenty-six-year-old university assistant in ethnology.

La Farge was in New Orleans when "North Is Black" was published. When he arrived in Cambridge in June, a member of the editorial staff of the Houghton Mifflin Company made an appointment to talk with him; he had read the story and had been impressed by both the style and the theme. The narrative thread dealt with the failure of a young Navajo guide to understand the society of whites into which a wealthy ranch woman had led him. The location of the ranch is north of the Navajo Reservation, a direction which in some of the Navajo mythology is held to be black and ominous. The story has a somber ending, as the Indian guide is rejected by a group that had at first accepted him. The Houghton Mifflin representative asked La Farge if he had thought of writing a book-length story of that type, and Oliver answered that he had begun a novel. Later, he received an invitation to send the finished manuscript to the publishing company, an invitation that was as good as a contract to the eager young writer. He returned to New Orleans where he completed, revised, and sent the manuscript in the mail. When the publisher accepted it, Oliver envisioned a sale of several thousand copies of *Laughing Boy*; but the book won the Pulitzer Prize for Fiction in 1930, and, after translation into a number of foreign languages, the ultimate sales are reported to have exceeded a quarter of a million copies.[6]

Few writers ever produced a more successful first novel. Very often, the first publication of a long narrative is stamped with the author's genius, but rarely does the book constitute his greatest artistic and commercial success; and *Laughing Boy* may have been both. The impact of quick popularity for this novel was both a triumph and a disaster for Oliver La Farge. Popularity as a writer catapulted him to fame, and it also betrayed the weakest side of his nature to his family and his friends: the aspect that fed on public acclaim, the spotlight, affluence, and cultural prestige. Oliver confesses that the artist in him disappeared in the flood of prosperity. The writer fled from New Orleans, which had been a creative well of inspiration for his early short stories and first book. The now prominent author moved to New York City with its great publishing houses and national magazines. La Farge returned to the city of his birth on a wave of triumph; but he began there what he considered the lost decade of his life, a decade almost fatal to his personal happiness and to his professional fulfillment.

# New York, 1930-1939

L A FARGE, who planned to lecture and write while in the metropolis, is listed on a brochure of the W. Colston Leigh Bureau at 521 Fifth Avenue, New York City, as available for talks on such subjects as "Facts in Fiction Writing," "The Rewards of Exploration," and "Indians as People." Under the first heading, he is quoted as saying: "I have few theories but many facts to discuss in this lecture." Among the facts listed are the urge to write, why it exists, and the justification for it; how and why he wrote *Laughing Boy*; how to write for big money and what it means. In the lecture on Indians, he discussed their differences from the white man; their humor, music, self-control, hospitality; and their potentials for civilization. The brochure proclaimed that the women in his audiences would take particular interest in the position Indian women held in their homes and in the social organization of their various tribes. Most of the listeners, he said, would be surprised to learn that, among the aborigines of America, the women owned the houses and all the furnishings. Husbands possessed only their personal apparel and weapons of warfare and hunting.

On September 28, 1929, Oliver La Farge was married to Wanden E. Mathews, who came from a socially prominent New England family, whose means and culture had provided travel for her in England, France, and Italy. She shared Oliver's interests in music, art, and literature. Although the marriage lasted eight years by the legal records, it really ended in six years, when a separation occurred. During the early, happy years, two children were born: Oliver Albee, on April 30, 1931, and Anya Povy, on August 17, 1933. "Anya Povy" is a Tewa Indian name, meaning "Sun Flower." Both the son and the daughter were born in New York City, where the La Farges lived in an apartment at 1088 Eighty-eighth Street, on the corner of Park Avenue. Wanden recalls that her husband did not give many lectures: "They fed him to the ladies luncheon clubs, and he got cranky about it. While trying to keep peace between the

ladies who wanted to pour and the ladies who wanted more personal details, the lecture got lost."[1]

## I  *Eastern Association on Indian Affairs*

From Oliver's own testimony, Wanden Mathews supplied him with the type of life a successful graduate of Groton and Harvard expected to enjoy. He dined with the socially elite on choice food and wines; a doorman at the fashionable apartment building kept out the newsboy and the traveling salesman; and an attendant with a breakfast tray cushioned the wear and tear of life. Wanden believed that this life was what Oliver desired and that the arrangement made possible his lecturing, administrative work, and writing.

In 1930 the headquarters of the Eastern Association on Indian Affairs was located in New York City. Hearing of La Farge's dedication to research and publication about Indians, a member of the association approached him about becoming a director of the group. After La Farge accepted, he went to Washington to sit with the United States Indian Commission while the members listened to reports on treaties, land rights, and state laws regarding Indians. The status of the first Americans from Alaska to Florida came into view. Advancement or decline of the American Indians depended to a great extent upon decisions made by the Bureau of Indian Affairs.

John Collier, the new commissioner, asked La Farge to conduct some investigations for the bureau. Four years later, La Farge was made field representative for the office (no longer bureau) of Indian Affairs. He also was appointed to the Advisory Committee on Arts and Crafts for the secretary of the interior. Many of these activities were not financially rewarding; to a considerable degree, they were supported by the financial resources of his wife.

## II  *Visit with the Newcombs*

Oliver and Wanden moved about a good deal; in the spring of 1930, they returned to the Navajo Reservation where they had spent their honeymoon in the previous fall. This time Oliver was investigating schools and checking on medical resources and sanitary conditions provided for teachers and children. Frances J. Newcomb,

42

whose husband Arthur owned the Blue Mesa trading post at Nava, New Mexico, recalls the La Farges at this time. She had first met Oliver in the late summer of 1924 when he had attended a ceremonial called "the Mountain Chant," which was held by Navajos in the Chuska Mountains eighteen miles west of Nava. The Newcombs had as guests Mary Cabot Wheelwright of Santa Fe and her cousin Lucy Cabot of Boston. As the group prepared to leave for the dance, a car stopped in the driveway. At the wheel was Alice Corbin Henderson, a well-known poet, who had moved from Chicago to Santa Fe in 1916. The second person in the car was her husband, William P. Henderson, an artist and architect; and their passenger was introduced as Oliver La Farge.

It was decided to lock the Henderson car in the Newcomb garage and for all to make the trip in the eight-passenger Buick of the Newcombs, which was already stocked with blankets, flashlights, and Thermos bottles of hot coffee and tea. Arthur Newcomb drove over sandy roads and up rocky slopes to the brush corral where Indian youths were dancing around a fire. Their bodies were painted with white clay, and their faces were striped with black coloring. They carried long whips of braided cedar bark. As the dance progressed, each thrust his whip into the flames and then lashed the clay-coated body of another dancer. La Farge was viewing the most spectacular of the Navajo rites for the first time. This, too, was his first meeting with Miss Wheelwright, whom he later assisted in studies of the Indian ceremonials and in plans for a museum in Santa Fe to preserve Navajo sand paintings and mythology.

Mrs. Newcomb describes Wanden La Farge as very charming and cordial: "She seemed small beside Oliver, and I was glad she did not wear levis or slacks, as these did not meet with the approval of the Navajos. She was very chic in a western-wear suit of a delft blue skirt and a jacket piped in red with a white blouse. A panama straw hat was tied down with a scarf which also protected her neck." She then described La Farge's appearance:

Oliver had taken up cowboy attire with a vengeance—black boots, blue levis one leg tucked into a boot; wide leather belt, plaid shirt, the inevitable red bandana tied under one ear, but no hat. His black hair (the color inherited from an Indian ancestor) was parted far to one side and combed straight and smooth over his head with the long ends in disorder. His book, *Laughing Boy*, had won the Pulitzer Prize and he was now working with a movie director to have it filmed. His trips to the

Reservation made it possible to assemble a cast of Navajo actors. It seems that the director would not work with Navajos who did not understand English. For young actors, there were plenty of school boys and girls, but for the next age group, not many educated couples were to be found. There were several in our valley and Arthur Newcomb offered to act as guide to the various hogans. I asked Wanden if she would care to stay at the Post while the men were gone, but she preferred going with them. I remember Arthur saying, "She is not letting her 'hero' very far from her sight." That amused me and I never forgot it. I believe they found one Indian family (man, wife, and two children) who would go to work for them.[2]

When the La Farges returned to New York in the late fall, Oliver was reading page proofs for two new books: one was *The Year Bearer's People*, in which he shared the honors of authorship with Douglas S. Byers, then at Andover Academy; the other was *Sparks Fly Upward*, a novel which turned the scientific data of *The Year Bearer's People* into fiction. La Farge said in the second Foreword written for *Laughing Boy* that he had fictionalized the knowledge acquired in writing his thesis for a master's degree.[3] In the same way, he made use of post-graduate study as background for *Sparks Fly Upward*.

III    *The Exposition of Indian Tribal Arts*

La Farge was willing to become almost radical when he envisioned changes needed to improve the status of Indians, whether in North, South, or Central America. In 1931, he helped organize the Exposition of Indian Tribal Arts, sponsored by the secretary of the interior and by the commissioner of Indian Affairs. The show was installed by Oliver's father and brother, Grant and Christopher La Farge. Exhibits in weaving, ceramics, metal, wood, bead work, and painting were obtained from collectors all over the United States. The exhibition, which opened on November 30, 1931, later toured the principal cities of the country. To explain and interpret the materials shown, the Brooklyn Museum published two handsomely illustrated booklets entitled *Introduction to American Indian Art*. The first was written by the artist John Sloan and Oliver La Farge: Sloan was president of the Exposition Board, and La Farge was a director. The second contained essays by twelve authorities on Indian poetry and arts.

In the year following the opening of this exposition, a merger occurred between the Eastern Association on Indian Affairs and the American Defense Association. La Farge was elected president of the new group, which was first named the American Indian Association and later, to avoid confusion with East Indian, the Association on American Indian Affairs. He held this position until the time of his death, except for the years he spent in the Army Air Transport Command.

Between 1930 and 1934, La Farge sold only seven stories, three of them to the *Saturday Evening Post*, and one each to *Scribner's*, the *Ladies Home Journal*, *Harper's Bazaar*, and *Esquire*. The financial return was not adequate to maintain his family at a Park Avenue scale of living. He dramatized *Laughing Boy* and attended rehearsals held by the Little Theater in New Orleans for the premiere on January 25, 1932.[4] In March of that year a Hollywood cameraman went to Arizona to film scenes near the Navajo Reservation for the cinema version of the book and play. A heavy snowfall on the high mesa country marooned the Indian communities, and the cameraman had to help rescue a group of Indians without making any footage for the picture.[5] Wanden Kane reports that William Wylder wanted to direct the film for Universal Studio and to make the picture as authentic as possible. He considered using shadows to portray the Navajo nature gods as they moved across the background. He asked Oliver to take a screen test for the leading role; but, since Oliver was not sufficiently histrionic or photogenic, Wylder decided to make him a technical assistant. Wanden was called in for advice on costuming. When she told a member of the wardrobe department that Navajo skirts required six-to-ten yards of material, the man said, "All right, but will they be sexy?" After failing to make the arrangements Wylder desired, he withdrew as director. Lew Ayres was under contract to Universal and was assigned the leading part, but the La Farges felt that he was miscast. Johnny Weismuller was also considered for the role of *Laughing Boy*, but cooler and saner heads prevailed. Ramon Novarro and Lupe Velez eventually were selected for the starring parts. La Farge, who was consulted in the early stages of the filming, decided not to watch the mutilation of his book and severed all connections with the movie-makers; he never saw a showing of the film.[6]

While the picture was having its first run, La Farge published his

third novel, *Long Pennant*, a title that refers to the flag of the *Glimpse*, a brig which becomes the stage for the opening scenes as a group of seamen from Chog's Cove, Rhode Island, sail down the Atlantic and into the Caribbean on a voyage which lasts for three years. According to Wanden, the book was not a financial success, and the failure to increase the family income deepened a crisis which was developing both in Oliver's writing and in his family life.

In the years before and after the publication of *Long Pennant*, Oliver was in Gallup, New Mexico, several times for the Inter-Tribal Indian Ceremonial. His recommendations with regard to this fair were favorably considered by the judges' committee at a meeting in Gallup on January 20, 1933.[7] Most of the Indians at this annual conclave were from the West. However, at the panel addressed by La Farge on April 17, 1934, in the ballroom of the Knights of Columbus Hotel, New York City, there were members from the Winnebago, Algonquin, Cherokee, and Sioux tribes along with the western Yakima and Hopi tribes. The subject Oliver discussed was the pending Wheeler-Howard Bill dealing with Indian rights.[8]

## IV  *Failure of a Marriage*

Oliver and Wanden came back to Santa Fe in the autumn of 1933, for he had decided that he wanted to live in the Southwest. They leased one of the fine old homes in the city and entered into the social life of the community of artists and writers. There were financial problems, and one of the children, Pete, had a mastoid infection. When Wanden took both of the children back to New York, Oliver followed, and he started his fourth novel, *The Enemy Gods*. His writing productivity increased between 1935 and 1938, and he found publishers among the best-known periodicals in the country. Most of the stories for these magazines were about Indians. An exception to the trend was a novelette *No More Bohemia*, for which he chose the New Orleans scene for color and motivation. He rewrote this story as his fifth novel seven years later.

Despite these active years, Oliver and Wanden were not happy in their marriage, for La Farge transferred the uncertainties of his writing career to his personal world. He was obviously disturbed that the Indian material he drew upon so freely would saturate his publishing market as it probably was saturating him. The experience of promoting the political, economic, and physical well-being of a

46

large cultural group through an association organized for that purpose was one thing; writing about the conflicts of these people for sale as fiction was something quite different. He was handling the problems of Indians all day and then perhaps writing about them all night to provide revenue for his family. As a result, the Indian as a source of creative imagination was running dry. Yet, as that resource diminished, his love for the Southwest grew; he wanted to return there—another element that contributed to the separation between him and Wanden.

During the spring of 1936, La Farge was in Santa Fe, as a sheet of La Fonda Hotel stationery dated May 25, 1936, testifies. On this writing paper he left the following jottings, giving them the title "The Epilogue," followed by the caption "Why They Come to Santa Fe":

> Because they have heard that between these
> mountains is the well where time lies
> still and yesterday's truth waits in
> naked beauty.
> The firewood smells like incense, adventure
> and ease lie down together, but above all
> leisure and contemplation survive.

A Santa Fe journalist had met Oliver in the hotel and had asked him to write "forty words" as the finishing touch for a book on Santa Fe. La Farge sat down and wrote exactly that number.[9]

Wanden obtained a divorce at Reno, Nevada, on August 27, 1937. Since they had been separated for two years, her decision was neither sudden nor surprising. In the fall of that same year, when La Farge went to the Southwest as a member of the Advisory Committee on Arts and Crafts appointed by the secretary of the interior, he met Consuelo Otille de Pendaries y Baca at a social event in Santa Fe. She was descended from one of the oldest Spanish families in New Mexico, a family which had landholdings northeast of Santa Fe near the headwaters of the Pecos River. This meeting was at fiesta time, and they met again when Consuelo went to New York that winter to visit her sister Emily, who was employed in the city. Oliver returned to Santa Fe in the summer of 1938, and that fall Consuelo worked in New York helping her friend Elizabeth Ingersol establish her office as a literary agent.

Consuelo and Oliver were married on October 14, 1939, in a Unitarian church. A reception followed at the apartment of his cousin, Oliver Claxton. Consuelo related that they went apartment hunting in Greenwich Village, somewhat to Oliver's alarm, since he had always lived Uptown. They found an attractive place at 19 West Tenth Street, a few doors from his grandfather's old studio. Oliver said that as a boy he would be asked "down" to visit with his grandfather, who would show him the brushes he used in painting, even allowing him to hold one and make a stroke with it.

## V  Santa Fe Becomes Home

Eight years separate *The Enemy Gods* from *Laughing Boy*, and two La Farges were involved in the writing of the novels. The first was the youthful explorer of an exotic mystical culture, one where racial strife and religious bigotry were unknown. The villagers drew upon the resources of nature which were influenced by rituals of poetic power. These people had never created city slums and grinding poverty. The novelist who wrote *Laughing Boy* saw the Indians as untouched by outside contacts and as living in a world of freedom and primitive beauty. The novelist who wrote *The Enemy Gods* was more realistic about this aboriginal Eden and more aware of the part such government agencies as Indian Affairs, Public Health, Forestry Service, and Reclamation Service play on Indian reservations.

In 1939, Miss Mary Wheelwright appointed La Farge a trustee for the Museum of Navajo Ceremonial Art in Santa Fe. She had founded this museum to preserve the unique heritage of myths, legends, and sand paintings of this Indian tribe. After first meeting Oliver at the Newcomb Trading Post in 1924, mutual interests led them to become close friends. He established contacts for the museum through the Association on American Indian Affairs; to serve the museum, he needed to live in Santa Fe. He also could move his office as president of the association there.

In the spring of 1940, the La Farges left New York City and rented a small house in Tesuque, a village which spreads along a tree-shaded canyon five miles north of New Mexico's capital. They stayed there until the fall of 1942, when Oliver left for the army. In the two and a half years they had lived at Tesuque, he had sold stories chiefly to *Esquire* and the *New Yorker*. Some were about his school days in New York and Massachusetts, and he discovered

that he did not have to live in either place to write about them.

Five of La Farge's novels were written before he moved to Santa Fe: *Laughing Boy* (1929), *Sparks Fly Upward* (1931), *Long Pennant* (1933), *No More Bohemia* (1935), rewritten as *The Copper Pot*; and *The Enemy Gods* (1937). Only *Cochise of Arizona*, which can be considered a juvenile, was completed after he left the East and the South. The first collection of short stories, *All the Young Men*, was published in 1935; and two outstanding scientific works and a monograph on Navajo spoken sounds also appeared before 1940, a total of nine books. After arriving in Santa Fe, La Farge wrote or edited fifteen more books (in three of which he had collaborators). This list included an autobiographical narrative, *Raw Material* (1945); two historical volumes, *War Below Zero* (1944), and *The Eagle in the Egg* (1949); another scientific work, *Santa Eulalia* (1947); a descriptive *Pictorial History of the American Indian* (1956); and two more collections of short stories, *A Pause in the Desert* (1957) and *The Door in the Wall* (posthumously published in 1964).

Clippings from the *Santa Fe New Mexican*, edited as *The Autobiography of a Southwestern Town* (1959), and selections from his column in the same newspaper, published as *The Man with the Calabash Pipe* (1966), fill out the period of accomplishment in the last twenty-three years of his life. The greater part of his fiction was written before he moved to the Southwest, and the greater part of his nonfiction was written afterward. His fame may rest upon one as much as upon the other.

# Santa Fe, 1940-1963

T HE SOUTHWEST OFFERED La Farge both a laboratory and an artistic outlet. The earliest studies he made of an ethnographic group, the Navajos, were made in Arizona. There and in New Mexico the Navajos were enclosed by Spanish and Anglo-American societies. The Indians were isolated and formed the only truly ethnological or racial community. The Spanish and the Anglo social groups were so intermingled that their societies were no longer either traditional or entirely uniform. La Farge believed that he had some kinship to the American Indians,[1] and he had married into the Spanish-American community. Furthermore, he was happier in a small city than in a metropolis. He states that he was pleased when people in Santa Fe stopped him on the street to tell him that they had enjoyed reading his books and articles. Even strangers sometimes introduced themselves to do the same thing. He said that New Yorkers were afraid of being thought unsophisticated if they expressed themselves as excited or as surprised by any accomplishment. He concluded that "a small town has warmth and rewards that big city dwellers never dream of."[2]

## I *League of American Writers*

Not long after the move to Santa Fe, Oliver became involved in a disturbance within the League of American Writers. This organization, founded in 1935, at one time numbered eight hundred members. One of the founders was Malcolm Cowley, who held the post of vice president from the date of organizing. Cowley, who had earned his baccalaureate degree from Harvard in the year before La Farge entered, had become a free-lance writer and, in 1929, associate editor of the *New Republic*. Accustomed to the play of ideas, he expected that an organization of writers in the United States would always be free to translate thought into action. When La Farge became a member of the executive committee of the league in 1937, he shared Cowley's conception of the organization. Nevertheless, both were surprised to discover that a well-

knit Marxist group had been formed in the league to support the Russo-German pact which was signed by Stalin and Hitler on August 24, 1939, and that this group was trying to win general support in the United States for a coalition of antidemocratic forces in Europe.

Cowley wrote to La Farge on July 31, 1940, enclosing a copy of the letter he had addressed to Franklin Folsom, executive secretary of the league. In the letter, Cowley protested two statements of policy made by officers which had led members to resign from the league: "I have disagreed rather violently with both statements, and have been deeply disturbed by the resignations." He added that the dispute was not one of personalities, politics, or Red-baiting; it was a disagreement about "what the war in Europe means, in the light of yesterday and tomorrow, and what steps this country should take to defend itself."[3] Since La Farge was one of those directors who had resigned after September, 1939, it is certain that he agreed with Cowley when he said that the war in Europe had become a battle to decide which types of human society should dominate the world: the dictatorships of the Nazi and Soviet types, or the free democracies which were being attacked. Hitler and Stalin proposed to abolish the American and French revolutions and to substitute the regimented state or the soviet for the rights of the individual. The course which the league was following seemed assured to weaken the power of the United States to resist fascism, nazism, and sovietism. Since the League of American Writers was doing more to destroy democracy than to defend it, Cowley chose to join the others who had resigned.

When Germany broke the Russo-German pact and invaded Russia on June 22, 1941, all the pro-German members of the league became anti-Russian, and all the pro-Russian members became anti-German. After Germany's ally, Japan, attacked the United States on December 7, 1941, no options were left for truly loyal American writers. The league was disbanded, retaining only the memories of its past confusions. Malcolm Cowley served with the wartime Office of Facts and Figures in Washington during 1942, and on September 12 of that year La Farge was commissioned as a captain in the Army Air Transport Command in which he served as a military historian until the end of the conflict.

Before he entered the armed forces, he saw his fifth novel in the bookstores. As previously stated, *The Copper Pot* is a rewritten

*No More Bohemia.* The chief characters (with some changes in naming) and the plot were lifted from the novelette with its setting in New Orleans.[4] However, the feeling for the painter's brush and the talk of artists may reflect Santa Fe in 1940 when artists were arriving to paint the southwestern sky so popularized by Maxfield Parrish—with distant mountains, white clouds, and blue distances. Painters were reproducing the scenes of Indian campfires and cowboy roundups for calendars and murals like the one painted by Tom Hartshorn, the hero of both *No More Bohemia* and *The Copper Pot.* The preliminary Note to *The Copper Pot* is signed "O. La F., Tesuque, New Mexico." The revision of the story must have been completed during the two years he had lived there. He was scheduled to join the Army Air Transport Command on September 12. His wife's mother entered the hospital several weeks before that time, and the La Farges moved into the Baca house at Santa Fe in order to be near her. When Oliver left, his friends went to say goodbye to him at Lamy, where Santa Feans board the Atchison, Topeka, and Santa Fe Railroad. They went around gathering wood to build a bonfire, and the farewell was accompanied by sparks, flame, and cheers appropriate to the occasion.

## II  *The Army Air Transport Command*

While La Farge was a member of the Air Transport Command, his wife served as a civilian employee in the same department. On March 2, 1943, Oliver became chief of the historical division. Under his direction were fifty full-time officers as well as additional enlisted persons and civilians. Many were stationed in Washington, but others were at far-flung outposts of the Army Air Force. Some two hundred and fifty more officers and men were assigned to army bases as part-time historians. The united efforts of this personnel produced fifty manuscript volumes of documents describing how the Air Transport Command developed from the Army Air Corps Ferrying Command, the Air Transport Association, certain supply services, and commercial training schools.

Three years after La Farge was mustered out of the army, he wrote *The Eagle in the Egg*, describing how air transport overcame the vast spaces which separated America from its Allies, and how the transport force grew within three and a half years from an odd assortment of one hundred and twenty twin-engine aircraft to one thousand four-engine and two thousand twin-engine transports,

not counting other minor and miscellaneous types of planes. Before La Farge left the Transport Command on August 30, 1946, he collaborated with a group of commissioned and noncommissioned officers in preparing another book dealing with this service. *War Below Zero* consisted of two long narratives and two very short ones, all of them telling of the hardships encountered in building and holding an Army Air Force base on the ice cap in Greenland.

Anyone who counts the pages written by an author so successful as La Farge begins to wonder where he found the time and energy to produce so much material. In the year following *War Below Zero*, and even before Oliver was separated from the Air Transport Command, his publishers issued *Raw Material*, the account he had written of the more important periods of his life. Of course, seven of the sixteen chapters in the book had been published previously in magazines; but nine new chapters were added, and these had to be written while he carried out his duties as chief of the Historical Division of the Transport Command. He states in the Foreword that he had received a Guggenheim Fellowship providing him with the leisure to write two books and that *Raw Material*, with new chapters, was in the planning stage before he entered the army in 1942; the other book was *The Eagle in the Egg*, which was not published until 1949.

### III  *647 College Street*

Upon returning to Santa Fe from Washington, D.C., in the fall of 1946, Oliver and Consuelo bought a house at 647 College Street, a street once the Old Pecos link in the Santa Fe Trail. The house was old, with thick adobe walls and high ceilings which were supported by exposed round log beams. The La Farges remodeled the house to provide an additional bedroom and a study, which later served also as an office for the Association on American Indian Affairs. The spacious living room had all the characteristics of the native New Mexican interior: white walls, deep-set windows, and Indian-style fireplace with a raised hearth. Personal touches were the bookcases flanking the chimney, two native drums near the couch, a coffee table holding a pottery bowl. On the wall, watercolor paintings by Indian artists added color to the white backgound; and a Persian rug in front of the couch harmonized with the Navajo rugs on each side of it.

54

The study, at the right front of the building, had two doors: one a solid Dutch door which served to ventilate as well as open to the north porch; the other, a French door which made possible a walk to the small porch on College Street. Both porches were supported by narrow columns not unrelated to colonial porches in New England, although the woodcraft of New Mexico made use of simpler tools to achieve an even more ornate effect. The walls of the study were of brown earth color; but the fireplace, with a low curving buttress, was white. Here, too, bookshelves extended from the raised hearth to the south corner where a combination tool bench and coffee bar was fitted out with pliers, saws, grass clippers, screw drivers, and a bit and auger, all suspended on a masonite punchboard. An electric percolator rested on two white boards, neighbor to Tender Leaf tea bags, a jar of powdered milk, saucers, coffee mugs, and cinnamon crackers. Over the typewriter, a Mexican wallhanging with designs in blue, green, and red decorated the north wall.

Here La Farge dictated professional letters sent as president of the Association on American Indian Affairs and as trustee of the Museum of Navajo Ceremonial Art. Here, too, he kept his scrapbooks, manuscripts, and mementos of the past, such as a small silver cup on the fireplace ledge. Emblazoned with the Groton shield, the inscription reads "*Cui servire est regnare,*" which may be translated freely as "To serve is to rule." The cup is lettered: "1st Squannacooks, 1920, O. La Farge, Capt. No. 4," which also requires translation. There were two rowing clubs at Groton, the Squannacook and the Hemenway; Oliver belonged to the first, which was named for a small stream on which the boys rowed. La Farge was captain of the First Squannacook Crew and rowed No. 4 in an eight-oared shell.[5] The other object which stirred memories was the semi-Windsor-type armchair, painted black with gold bands on the rungs and adorned with a gilded shield holding the word "*Ve-ri-tas*" lettered on an open book surrounded by a laurel wreath. This Harvard University seal places the ideal of truth before all of its graduates. What a range of verities are encompassed by the motto. How can the truth in economic necessities, emotional compulsions, material, and psychological pressures be measured in individuals and groups? Integrity in the search for truth may be the key to anyone's success or failure. Oliver La Farge faced that challenge in everything he wrote.

## IV  *The Guitar Club*

Oliver and Consuelo became charter members of the Santa Fe Guitar Club when it was organized in 1949. There were a dozen members, all qualified in some degree to perform on the guitar. In addition, the group selected two honorary members because they were admirers of the instrument rather than players of it. Meetings combined the pleasures of both social and musical assembly. A photograph made in November, 1949, shows La Farge seated in the front row on the floor; he is not holding an instrument, but Consuelo, seated on a chair in the second row, holds a guitar on her lap. When, on January, 8, 1950, the club sponsored a recital by Carlos Montoya, Oliver was so stirred by the performance that he wrote in his weekly column for the *Santa Fe New Mexican* the following comments:

> I have heard Montoya, and I look forward to hearing him again with real eagerness combined with a touch of dread. The dread is because an hour of his intense, whirling, terrific music leaves you a little weak, a trifle gasping.
> He is a small man with beautiful hands. He seems not much bigger than his concert guitar when he bends over it. . . . The speed of his fingers is unbelievable. The things he does to the strings are plain unlawful. It is incredible that gut or nylon could stand the treatment. There are moments in the really exciting passages, the ones that make you want to cut loose and shout "Olé," when it seems as if the only thing left for him to do was bend the instrument double and you believe he could if he wanted to.
> That's the effect Montoya has on people. It's in him, in his playing, and in the Flamenco music, that strange, fiery, complicated nostalgic blend of ancient Gypsy, Moorish, and European form. It lies behind the heritage of all the Spanish speaking Americas. . . .[6]

## V  The White Shell Cross

Early in 1951, the directors of the Tucson Festival of the Arts began preparations to stage *The White Shell Cross*, a drama written by La Farge with dances arranged by the choreographer Letitia Evans. The musical scores were prepared by Robert Parris, and the entire spectacle was directed by Peter R. Marroney. The cast numbered fifty-four actors and dancers who were accompanied by a chorus of fifty-two voices and an orchestra of seventeen musicians.

The University of Arizona stadium was used for the performance, and a stage eighty feet wide and sixty feet deep was constructed on two levels. The upper level at the rear made possible a presentation of the Blessed Virgin and her foe, the Indian goddess, after the White Shell Cross had been stolen by Hunter Indians. Below this stage, another level was used for the activities of human beings who appeared in twenty-four scenes mounted on circular platforms. Thirty-four screens were set up as backdrops. The plot portrayed struggles between planter Indians and Spanish settlers who were attacked by pagan hunter Indians aided by barbarous American mountain men. However, one of the mountain men is modeled on Kit Carson and is hero of the plot. The pagan and Christian powers helped to restore harmony at the last to the accompaniment of Spanish liturgical music.[7]

### VI   *The Society for Applied Anthropology*

In the summer of 1951, the Society for Applied Anthropology, of which La Farge was a member, printed a "Code of Ethics" in its publication *Human Organization*. The declaration was to serve as a guide for the social scientists who belonged to the organization. After reading the document, Oliver wrote to the editor on October 27, 1951, to voice his vigorous dissent and to ask that his letter be published. Before taking such action, the editor sent the letter to Dr. Margaret Mead, eminent author and anthropologist, who had acted as chairman of the committee which drew up the code. As a basis for his protest, Oliver referred to the "verbose, roundabout" character of the language, which he called so "self-cancelling and inadequate" as to remove the scientist from any responsibility for his words or actions if either should be questioned.

After reading the letter, Miss Mead replied on December 12 with an explanation of the difficulties in drawing up a statement which would define the ethical matters involved and also reconcile divergent points of view. After admitting that the literary style was cumbersome, she requested La Farge to rewrite the statement and to use "simple and beautiful English" if he could do so without sacrificing the fundamentals expressed. On January 15, 1952, Oliver answered that he felt helpless to improve it because two intentions were confused in the declaration: one was a positive moral position about supplying anthropological knowledge to society; the other, a statement about the responsibility of a scientist to accept the conse-

quences of such information if it were put to use with an unfortunate outcome. He repeated his belief that the "Code of Ethics" was too cautious and self-protective to achieve the end for which it was intended. In the final letter he wrote, couched in less extreme terms, he expressed a high opinion of the chairman of the committee as a writer and as a scientist.[8]

## VII   *The Santa Fe "Bird-Watcher"*

On January 8, 1951, La Farge wrote his first column for the Sunday edition of the *Santa Fe New Mexican*. It was called "The Santa Fe 'Bird-Watcher' " in reference to the on-looker watching birds, but the implication is clear that all the birds, watcher and watched, are people. With only a few exceptions, this column appeared until within two weeks of the author's death. On December 28, of that first year of the column, John Pendaries La Farge was born; and, a year later, his father commemorated that event by writing in the column that it had been a custom in his family to read the "Gospel of St. Luke" at this season to dramatize the enchantment which every child brings to Christmas Day. Oliver, who had celebrated his own fiftieth birthday seven days before "Penny" was born, commented that in a few years his son would discover what his father had to learn: "being born so close to Christmas is a gyp."[9]

Life at 647 College Street was composed of many activities: dictating during office hours with interruptions for conference with officials of the association; regular periods at the typewriter writing short stories and articles; visits from Indian friends, chiefly those from the Pueblo tribes since contacts with the Navajos had practically ceased; and regular trips to New York City to visit with members of the La Farge family and to attend meetings at the association headquarters. Although no more full-fledged novels formed in his mind, La Farge wrote two juveniles—*Cochise of Arizona* (1953) and *The Mother Ditch* (1955)—and also a story of Spanish-American life, *Behind the Mountains* (1956). The short stories written (some of them published) between 1936 and 1954 appeared in *A Pause in the Desert* (1957); those between 1957 and 1963, in *The Door in the Wall* (1965).

## VIII   *The* "Quién Sabe?" *Club*

A group of Santa Fe men in 1954 organized the "*Quién Sabe?*" Club, with a name as informal as the structure of the club. "*Quién*

*Sabe?"* may be translated as "Who knows?" or "Who knows anything?"; and there were no officers, no constitution, no bylaws, no set programs. The members simply agreed to meet on the first Friday of each month at the house of one member; and, after a supper provided by the host (with the help of his wife), somebody volunteered an opinion which was challenged and then discussed. After the discussion, beverages, song, and diversion of one sort or another followed for the remainder of the evening. By common agreement, 60 percent of the membership had to be engaged in the arts, a warranty that politics and business had to take second place to the more literary and philosophic interests of a majority in the club. Oliver was one of the founders, and after his death a friend stated that the club declined somewhat in spirit. This friend, who was a painter and a silversmith, declared: "When he made a friend, he was capable of the deepest friendship known. He was a lovable man."[10] Not everyone agreed with the adjective "lovable" chosen by this friend, for through his column La Farge angered people with commerical interests and those who were trying to modernize Santa Fe. He never agreed that modernity was a substitute for the beauty and charm found in the older sections of the town.

Secretary of the Interior Stewart L. Udall announced in the summer of 1961 a plan to convert the Santa Fe Indian School into an Institute of American Indian Arts. He felt that an educational center was needed where Indian children could develop their talents for painting, sculpture, weaving, and ceramics. When opposition to the proposal developed among both Indians and whites, La Farge was surprised. A number of the Indian leaders called the new facility "a useless unwanted school for the 'arts elite.' " They preferred a more vocational emphasis; others insisted upon retaining the standard preparatory school. La Farge pointed out that the selected Indian children who attended the institute would be given the standard high school curriculum with a diploma and then two years of applied arts, which would prepare them for specialized fields of employment. Most of those who had previously been in attendance were being sent to public schools near their home villages. After further discussion, the institute was approved and became a success, but idealists among the non-Indian artists and craftsmen had discovered that there were as many Indian as white parents who preferred their offspring to be taught more "practical" skills than the use of paintbrushes and sculptors' tools.[11]

## IX  *Operation for Emphysema*

Early in 1957, La Farge had experienced difficulty in breathing. He smoked cigarettes constantly and knew that his lungs were congested. At the Lovelace Clinic in Albuquerque, his illness was diagnosed as emphysema. After a few days at Bataan Memorial Hospital, he had the infected tissue removed from his right lung; the infection was arrested, and he regained his strength when he returned to Santa Fe. A letter from the novelist Paul Horgan on June 8, 1957, mentions this illness but urges Oliver to give lectures on the novel at a Writers' Workshop planned by the University of Iowa for the following year. Oliver stopped using tobacco and limited his alcoholic drinks to an occasional glass of wine, usually sherry. He went to California and felt so well he started smoking again.

During every illness, he never abandoned the hours of work for the Association on American Indian Affairs, nor did he diminish the time devoted to his writing. In the two winters that followed the lung operation, he survived spells of virus pneumonia. He needed a long rest, but the Taos Indians were just beginning their legal battle to reclaim lands that had been theirs before and after Europeans had first occupied the area around their pueblo. A Spanish governor had issued a title to them in 1793 (recognizing possession which had been reported by members of the Coronado expedition in 1540). The Spanish title was confirmed by the United States surveyor general on December 22, 1858. Since that date the Bureau of Biological Survey and the National Forest System had induced the Pueblo of Taos to permit grazing and recreational activities on the range and in the timber country. Northeast of the pueblo were shrines and lakes held sacred by the Indian religion; but the lakes were invaded by fishermen, and the shrines were littered with debris cast away by campers. Oliver states the case for the Taoseños in an article he wrote for his newspaper column on July 31, 1961.

In 1909 and again in 1918, the director of the Forest Service assured the Indians of Taos that their rights would be protected. An Act of Congress in 1933 specified that the pueblo should have the use of thirty-two thousand acres through a fifty-year period and retain exclusive possession of the land around Blue Lake in August when the religious ceremonies took place. Recreationers continued to violate these guarantees, and in 1953 the attorneys for the pueblo appeared before the Indian Claims Commission to ask that the area

be protected and that the tribe be compensated for years in which others had been allowed to use it.[12] A decision by the commission had been ten years in the making when Oliver was preparing to go east in 1963 for the annual meeting of the association.

He went to Taos to try to stop the Forestry Service from issuing permits for summer fishing and camping on pueblo land. The snow had not yet melted, and the air was very cold. Feverish and coughing, he returned to Santa Fe to recover before leaving for New York City. He corresponded before the meeting with Edna Ferber, who wrote to him on May 2 about her interest in the Indians of southern Arizona. While in the East, La Farge also had an engagement at Harvard University, where he had been invited to serve as a judge for some boat races. He had to sit in a racing shell on a cold, wet day while the contest was decided. When he came back to the Harvard Yard, where an apartment had been reserved for him, there was no heat in the building. Streams of people came in, all with hospitable greetings for a distinguished alumnus who was, in fact, exhausted and sick, but determined to stay on his feet in order to acknowledge their friendly welcome. He could scarcely walk up the stairs to his bedroom. He returned to Santa Fe so weakened that his lung collapsed.

On July 24, 1963, he again entered Bataan Hospital, where he was attended by the same doctor who had performed the resection on his lung six years before. The surgeon found that the lung had hemorrhaged and that surgery to clear the tissues was again necessary. The shock of this second operation was too great for a heart already weakened by the strain of heavy breathing. He died on Friday, August 2, at three o'clock in the afternoon.[13] Consuelo was with her husband at the hospital, as were Pete and Povy. La Farge was too weak to see any of them but Consuelo.

## X   *Final Ceremony*

The funeral rites were scheduled for Monday morning, August 5, at the Episcopal Church of the Holy Faith in Santa Fe. On that morning, the governor of Taos Pueblo and his chief assistant came to 647 College Street before the ceremony. When Consuelo met them at the door, she knew from what they said that there were more Indians waiting outside in automobiles. When she asked them all to come into the house, the living room was filled with the crowd. Several Indians spoke; and, as what they said was translated to her,

the meaning was beautiful. All of the Taos group went to the church and occupied the front pews. A large number returned to the house afterward, sitting around formally and being served coffee. There was little conversation.

Oliver La Farge, though a professed Christian, held a type of pantheistic belief in man as subject to the forces of nature. He thought that the rituals of all religions and the explanations behind them were the product of early stages of human knowledge; but he also recognized that in religious conviction lay spiritual values which should be respected whether in primitive or in advanced forms of belief. Behind the superstition and taboos of the Navajo worship of nature lay the ideals of beauty and harmony expressed by their word *hozhoni*, a state of spiritual peace which they tried to reach through prayers, dancing, song, and sand paintings.

Nothing in either Christian or Indian belief convinced him that "Oliver La Farge," that inner essence of identity, would continue as such.[14] Yet he believed in a power outside man and did not reject the concept of God. Persons of many faiths attended his funeral, among them those of national as well as local prominence. Interment was in National Cemetery at Santa Fe. Honorary pallbearers included the secretary of the interior, the commissioner of Indian Affairs, several former secretaries of these government agencies, a Pulitzer Prize-winning author, and representatives of the Miccosukee Seminole tribe, the Cheyenne tribe, and the All-Pueblo Council of New Mexico.[15]

# Part II

# WRITER OF FICTION

A writer with a notebook is comparable to a painter using a camera for his preliminary studies. Good writing stems from things so deeply felt, so sharply perceived, that they are unforgettable.

If an artist doesn't change, he deteriorates; there is no such thing as remaining at a fixed level.

It is characteristic of Indians when not under overwhelming pressure that they never lose sight of the great fundamental question: What makes life worth living?

. . . if you have an idea for a novel . . . everything else will revolve about this for six months or more; you will eat, breathe, and sleep it, think of it at odd times, and find all other interests completely dominated by the idea of the complete job—and wonder what the completed job will be like.

—From *Raw Material*
(Used with permission)

# New Worlds in View: Novels

L A FARGE ENTERED the Indian world, as his ancestors had when they came to New England, seeking new horizons. He learned from his father about the early inhabitants around Narragansett Bay. He read about their folklore and then was sent to study a different sort of Indian whose ancient life was still visible in the cliff dwellings and in the huge communal apartment houses of the Southwest. He linked the contemporary Mayans of Central America with their jungle-surrounded temples and paved courtyards. With his literary temperament and anthropological training, how could he escape the desire to make the world of early America live through fiction?

## I Laughing Boy

"Sings Before Spears" is the sacred or ceremonial name of the hero in La Farge's first novel, but the reader does not learn his name until the sixth chapter of *Laughing Boy*. Then, both the hero's sacred name and that of the heroine, Slim Girl, are revealed. She is called "Came with War," in accord with the Navajo custom of giving a warlike name to a child, especially to a girl. The identifications for the couple previously in use are those describing a habit or physical trait, as illustrated by "Laughing Boy" and "Slim Girl." Both these nicknames, as well as the sacred names, are a kind of orientation for the reader, introducing him into a world as close to the spear and the bow as it was to ceremonies sung for good health, harvest, and hunting. All four of the names mark contrasts between a simple Navajo way of life and the complex American civilization which surrounded the Indian Reservation.

Into the sunshine and mesa-rimmed landscape of northern Arizona, the reader rides with Laughing Boy, who is guiding his horse to a Navajo Mountain Chant where dancing, singing, racing, feast-

ing, even gambling are a part of a religious festival. Scores of people will be there, but almost everyone will know everyone else, either as a relative or as a friend. The Navajos were like a family grown into a tribe, or a tribe living like a family, with the gap between rich and poor too narrow to arouse either greed or envy. The faults of men were there, but Laughing Boy had never heard of a jail; and, when he is told what such a place is like, he decides that he would rather be dead than ever see the inside of one.

The novelist published his first poetry as "Three Indian Chants," which were printed in the *Harvard Advocate* during April, 1923; and he wrote his "Baccalaureate Hymn" in the following year. Eighteen years later he submitted "Draft Names Drawn" to the *Saturday Review of Literature* and saw it printed on March 8, 1941. Yet the reader of *Laughing Boy* recognizes the novelist as a poet in the first chapter when Sings Before Spears looks across the flare of light from the bonfire and sees Slim Girl in her blue velveteen blouse decorated with ceremonial silver. She is standing with a group of women, and the sight of her causes Laughing Boy to join in the singing, hoping to attract her attention. He does not see her again until she tugs at his blanket to draw him into the dance, addressing him with a Navajo term that is caressing. She pulls him forward, and they dance while the pounding of the drums and the chorus of male voices creates a mood in the firelight under a summer moon. The book has begun with a curing ceremony held in warm weather, and it ends eighteen months later with the Night Chant, which is held only in the fall or winter. This outward sequence of season and ceremony matches the inner story, as the relationships between the protagonists acquire intensity. The plot becomes more complex for Slim Girl as she moves between the world of the white man and the Indian. Laughing Boy moves in the Indian world alone; and, until the book ends, he has greater need of healing than she does.

After the two young people have first met at the Squaw Dance, Laughing Boy wins a bet in a wrestling match, and he sells the belt of silver plaques he has made. He also wins the prize at a horse race, but all of his loot is lost when he gambles with an Indian called Red Man who knows Slim Girl. After the gambling, Laughing Boy meets Slim Girl at a spring. When she persuades him to leave with her, they go to the hogan she has built near the railroad tracks. He refuses to sleep inside the earth-covered lodge until a medicine man has made prayers over them. Slim Girl bribes a medicine man to

marry them in return for whiskey which she had obtained from a white rancher, who had given her money and whiskey for weekly appointments at her hogan. After the marriage, the Indian couple live at Laughing Boy's hogan on the reservation where he works as a silversmith, and she takes his silver to the curio shop near the railroad. However, she continues her weekly appointments at her hogan, explaining to Laughing Boy that she stays in town to work for the wife of a missionary who befriended her after the death of her parents. She tells the rancher, who is a widower, that she has a drunken old man for a husband and that she needs liquor to keep him contented.

As the plot develops, it probes both Indian and white attitudes toward love and marriage. Few Indians have written about love, and what has been reported by white social scientists records the Navajo reticence about pre-marital socializing among their young people. Aside from ceremonial dancing and the ritualistic visits of the two families before a marriage agreement, Indian young people have little freedom to mingle socially. The parents of both Laughing Boy and Slim Girl were dead; therefore, the formalities between them were personal rather than tribal. Slim Girl had worked in the household of a white missionary, but she had been seduced by a white cowboy; and, after leaving the home of the missionary, she had been in a house of prostitution where she had met the white rancher. The problem of the novelist in dealing with the love affair between Laughing Boy and Slim Girl was to adjust their behavior to both Indian and white backgrounds. During the brief courtship between the two Navajos, Laughing Boy never kissed Slim Girl because he did not know what a kiss was. After she gave him whiskey at the wedding feast, she initiated her husband into the type of embrace she had learned from her white lovers.

There is no word in Navajo for "romance"; for "love," the Navajos make use of the term for "best" plus the term for sexual intercourse. No words in Navajo contain the overtones of romance which have been added to sexual attraction by the European code of romantic love developed by courtly and religious mysticism. Therefore, the second half of *Laughing Boy* is written with an aura of psychology more familiar to a white reader than to an Indian. Polygamy was permitted in Navajo life if a widowed man desired to marry his wife's sister or perhaps another relative. Women, however, were not allowed more than one husband; and, until the advent

of American law, adultery was punished by the amputation of an eye, an ear, or the nose. Today, divorce is possible although it is not common or approved.[1]

The relatives of Laughing Boy do not accept Slim Girl into their family group. Although she attends Navajo ceremonies and wears the dress of the tribe, she changes her clothing when she goes to the curio shop or to keep her rendezvous with the rancher. As her married life becomes routine, she believes that she is revenging herself upon all white people by using the rancher's money to make a better life for her Navajo husband and herself. They are prosperous: the corn ripens, and the peach trees bear fruit; the loom before the door fills as Slim Girl weaves. But Laughing Boy is not happy; he and his wife are not a part of the Navajo community even though they attend the ceremonies. There have been no children. He does not like the look on Slim Girl's face when she returns from her visits to the American town. To cure his restlessness, he goes in search of a lost horse. After four days of wandering, he finds the horse and is returning home through the American town where he believes Slim Girl is staying with the missionary's wife. As he passes a house on the edge of town, he looks through a window and sees his wife with a man. When the man runs outside, Laughing Boy wounds him with an arrow. When Slim Girl appears, he shoots an arrow through her arm.

After they return to Laughing Boy's hogan, he removes the arrow and binds her wound. She tells him of her past life, explaining the necessity for what she has done. She convinces him that she wants only to go with him into the northern part of the reservation and to live where there are no white Americans. When her arm has healed, they gather their possessions and start for an unclaimed fertile strip where even in dry summers there is water. The day is not far gone as they ride into a canyon and are observed by the Navajo called Red Man, who has known about Slim Girl's past life. He remembers how Laughing Boy defeated him in wrestling and racing; he also harbors resentment against Slim Girl for never having favored him. He draws his rifle from the saddle and fires three shots, then ducks behind a low rock in the canyon before riding away. Slim Girl slumps forward, and Laughing Boy supports her as best he can until they are able to turn the horses and stop. Then he builds a fire and tries to make her comfortable on a couch of blankets. She speaks of their marriage as having restored her as

a Navajo, and she makes him promise not to seek her slayer for revenge. Laughing Boy makes this promise before she dies in his arms.

Thirteen years after the novel was published, La Farge referred to this scene as a "purple" passage, as one overly emotional in treatment.[2] He stated that he was guilty of transferring his own emotions to Laughing Boy and that he perhaps had lacked the self-discipline necessary to tone down the climax of his story. Yet his problem was greater than the writing of any single scene in the novel. His problem was to make a character like Slim Girl believable: an Indian who knew the best and the worst types of people in both red and white races and to whom the Navajo way of life had become an eddy in the stream she drifted in, not the main current. Crossing this gap, one both physiological and psychological, would be a challenge to any writer's style and imagination. La Farge did it with remarkable success.

After Laughing Boy has prepared a grave for Slim Girl in a rocky niche, he covers her body with blankets; the weaving tools she had used; and the jewelery she had worn plus his own bow guard and belt of silver; then he mourns four days outside the wall while the snow falls and ice forms on the stunted trees. Finally, he seeks the place where the Navajos have gathered to hear the Night Chant. Now it is the spring of the second year he has lived with Slim Girl. He needs to renew his faith in the words *hohoji, hozhonae*: "renewal" and "beauty"; "let all be beautiful." As he joins the people around the bonfire within the circle of cedar branches, he sees the leader of the dancers holding prayer plumes and the young men lifting painted arrows which they appear to swallow and then live again. A sense of peace pervades him as the men dance through the flames and survive the fire. He is cleansed as they are, and he feels that now he is not alone.

In writing *Laughing Boy*, La Farge created a hero freed from such complications as existed in his own background and personality. Sings Before Spears had no history of preparatory school or college to help establish his fame and fortune. His education was limited to mastery of horses, to skill with bow and arrow, to stamina of body for wrestling, and to techniques for cutting, bending, or hammering silver to make bow guards and plaques for belts. He had no social standing to emulate or forswear. His cotton trousers, velveteen blouse, and leather moccasins met all the requirements for either formal or informal attire; and his bedroll with knapsack was all

the luggage he needed to travel. The hero of the novel thus became a cleansing or catharsis for the author as the Navajo follows a charted course in the book. A reader, too, may lose the restraints in his life as he moves into the open world of Navajoland.

Freedom or constraint in the life of a Navajo was related to the mythology of the tribe, especially to the search for a trail of beauty which ended in peace and harmony for the individual and those around him. Laughing Boy desired to walk this trail with Slim Girl. He could not walk it alone, and he urged his wife to attend the Night Chant so that they could take the first steps together. She agreed, although she did not feel at home with his relatives. At the Night Chant, Slim Girl joined the women in preparing ceremonial foods. The atmostphere of *hozhonae*, "happiness and beauty," pervaded her mind. By what she saw and did she began to walk in beauty; but the trail was long; and mountains, chasms, and barren spaces of omission and commission were in her path. She spoke to Sings Before Spears on the fifth afternoon of the ceremony when she found him concentrating on the Holy Things. At that moment, she became only a part of his world, not the center, nor the whole of it, as she had believed to be the fact.[3]

This "oneness" or "wholeness" shaped by Navajo thought was a remedy for the feeling of "separateness" in La Farge. He felt great need to join with others when he was at Groton Preparatory School. He found "oneness" when he became a member of the crew that moved their oars together in the eight-oared shell at Harvard. He tells of sitting up all night to pray and sing with Hopi Indians who were rehearsing for a Cloud Dance. When he first came into the kiva where the Indians were practicing, he sat down between an auto-repair man and a road-construction foreman. One called him by name, and the other handed him a cigar. He joined both in singing; and, as the Indians filled the council chamber with music, he felt communion with them. He called the night a "true approach to God."[4] Midway in his autobiographical narrative *Raw Material*, La Farge reveals that he never became a convert to the Navajo religion; but he states that "it showed me the way out of desolation." In the final chapter of *Raw Material*, he restates this need for group unity in a harmonious society; but he adds that such loyalty must be joined with the equal requirement of individual freedom in order to provide adequate "spiritual vitamins" for daily living.[5]

The unifying associations in the landscape surrounding *Laughing Boy* have a quality unique to the Navajos. Their world is bounded by four Sacred Mountains from which the gods in the Night Chant descend (even though human beings wear their masks and appear in their garments). Sings Before Spears takes his wife on a trip to legendary ruins where the Ancient People and the Divine Ones were said to have talked. He also rides with her to a high cliff where he points to the mountains in which the gods make their homes. Slim Girl is finally persuaded by these sights and sounds; and the division in her mind is cleared, as is the sickness in her spirit. Native traditions reclaim the defectress, and she returns to the tribe. Apostasy is thus condemned; but perhaps La Farge's answer to the charge of defection from his own environment would be that an ethnologist is at home anywhere; furthermore, he claimed to be part Indian in his New England tradition.

If a critic is to judge La Farge novels by the success of his style, the judgment might be formed on a standard proposed by the author himself: it is the test of monosyllabic words used to bring the sentences to life in descriptive or narrative scenes. He entitles his "Bird-Watcher" column on October 29, 1950: "If You Simply Must Write, Stick to the Monosyllables." In that Sunday article, he discusses the difference between spoken and written speech, pointing out that written words rely entirely upon one faculty or sense, the capacity of a person to see; but spoken words make use of several senses, that of hearing as well as seeing, perhaps even the sense of touch or that of smell. In the column, La Farge refers to Hemingway specifically as master of dialogue, an indication that in stressing monosyllables as effective in style La Farge had in mind the writing of fiction. Monosyllables on a written page are more likely to build imagery than are polysyllables. The "test of monosyllables" can be applied to any literary work by establishing the ratio of one-syllable words to those of more than one syllable by counting both on the page and determining the percentages. Since La Farge in his column mentioned Hemingway, the "test of monosyllables" is shown in the following chart, as applied to one thousand words in books written by La Farge and by Hemingway in the same year and to a book written by Steinbeck ten years later.

A monosyllabic test cannot be considered absolute since special types of dialogue and unusual types of character make demands

## THE TEST OF MONOSYLLABLES
### (as Applied to Novels by La Farge, Hemingway, and Steinbeck)

| Novel | Total lines | Total words | Percent Mono-syllabic | Percent Multisyllabic |
|---|---|---|---|---|
| Laughing Boy (1929) | 121 | 1000 | 73.8 | 26.2 |
| A Farewell to Arms (1929) | 102 | 1000 | 78.2 | 21.8 |
| The Grapes of Wrath (1939) | 105 | 1000 | 80.3 | 19.7 |

upon style which change the monosyllabic ratio. The test, however, is objective and does permit an appraisal of a writer's use of English, a language notable for its monosyllabic character. The other novels by La Farge have a higher percentage of multisyllabic words, which may shed light upon the material used and the characters presented.

## II   Sparks Fly Upward

La Farge wrote *Sparks Fly Upward,* his second novel, while he was reading proof for *The Year Bearer's People,* a scientific study of the Indian tribes in Guatemala which was completed after the Third Tulanc Expedition during the spring of 1927. In the second Foreword which the novelist wrote for *Laughing Boy* in the printing of 1962, he stated that he had fictionalized the knowledge he had acquired in writing a thesis for his master of art's degree.[6] He could have written a Foreword to introduce *Sparks Fly Upward* in which he announced that:

In Guatemala, while I was carrying on ethnological research, I found three social groups. The first was made up of Indians, who were en-slaved, despised, and resentful. At the top of the social scale was another group who were the Spanish aristocrats. They owned most of the land and they controlled the Army. In between the two strata were the *ladinos,* a large society of mixed bloods who ran the shops and small factories; they also filled the lesser offices in Church, State, and Army. My sympathies were with the lowest class of all, but my sense of plot developed from the conflict between the middle group and both the others. Here I found the hero for my novel. I gave him the name Esteban de Cerromayor, although he was really Esteban Perez y Bagil: Esteban Perez for his Spanish father and Bagil for his Indian mother. Cerromayor was his patron whom his mother saved from death on the battlefield where her husband was slain in the civil war between the *hidalgos* and the rebels. The personal side of the polit-ical struggle I dramatized with a love affair between Esteban, the

72

*ladino*, and Doña Favia, the aristocratic wife of Don Geronimo de Cerromayor. This book became important to me because in writing the novel I noticed a change in myself. I was slowly, unwittingly, turning into a liberal.[7]

In *Sparks Fly Upward*, the historic period is the first half of the nineteenth century when social change was occurring throughout Mexico and Central America. After Mexico had won independence from Spain in 1821, Guatemala and Honduras were also freed from the rule of a European monarchy, and they began their own search for democratic institutions. Through the influence of his foster father, Esteban Perez gains a commission in the army of the Republic of Alturas which, like many of the Latin American republics, found a new government by middle-class families as repressive as the monarchy had been. Esteban Perez lives with an Indian woman who bears him a son. In choosing between the revolution and the government, he sides with the intellectual leaders of the revolt, the *liberalistas*, and the downtrodden minorities. As a brigadier general, he leads the regiments under his command against the army of the *guardia* of the president and puts it to flight. Then the rebellion triumphs and Esteban rides beside the new patriots and their leaders. If there is a philosophy larger than the politics behind the actions of Esteban, he expresses it in these thoughts: "A man was not yet shaped for himself, or for any person, but for uses greater than all persons. Yes, he had thought, up there in the mountains, that a man has no will, but that was the torture of it—God made him and shaped him, put a use on him, and gave him a will of his own to tear him into pieces."[8]

The style used by La Farge in *Sparks Fly Upward* is almost as monosyllabic as that of *Laughing Boy*: he made use of 73.1 percent monosyllabic words in writing his second novel. Passages of great descriptive power hold interest when the plot lags. Two of these passages deal with the appearance and the symbolism accorded to the horses of principal characters. Doña Favia, the beautiful aristocrat, rides a creamy-brown mare, one with a cream-colored mane and tail. The soft, lively eyes have a winning expression that indicates a spirited but docile horse which has been well trained. In contrast, the hero Esteban gentles a wild, black stallion who matches his own surging passion, which he also pits against that of the horse. La Farge describes the battle between horse and man,

each of them half-tamed and determined to dominate the other. The horse was a three-year-old born in an upland meadow. As Esteban mounts, he throws away his sombrero and tightens his sash before the men snatch away the blindfold and the horse rises under him:

> It was caught in some kind of trap, things bound it, like the day it was roped and brought in, something heavy was on its back. It lunged forward, but the bindings and the weight came with it, offering no resistance. It could not brush past the ropes that bound its head, it twisted and nothing happened. Then there was hot pain, spurs thrust into its flanks, the stinging quirt on its quarters, and yells from the men standing about. The thing on top was screeching and clawing like a wildcat, only the horse knew it was a man. It twisted itself once like a snake, then it leaped high into the air and came down stiff-legged. As it continued bucking, its fighting spirit returned, twisting on itself, lashing out forefeet and hind, leaping and turning in the air, all one wild passion of fury that was close kin to panic.[9]

His stepfather and Doña Favia watch Esteban in his conquest of the horse, but Esteban accepts the name Ek Ahau, "Black Captain," given to the horse by the Indians; and the horse appears to dominate the master as it carries him to victory in the civil war. Esteban talks to Ek Ahau in Rashti, the Indian speech, an unconscious gesture to the Indian cause in the revolution and a symbol of the choice Esteban made.[10]

### III   Long Pennant

La Farge wrote a novel every two years between 1929 and 1933. In *Long Pennant*, all the staging areas are familiar to him: the first was Chog's Cove, Rhode Island, a real place with an invented name;[11] the second, the coastline of southern Mexico or Guatemala; the third, New Orleans. The characters in the cast are New Englanders who sail in the *Glimpse* down the Atlantic and into the Caribbean on a voyage which lasts for three years. When the ship overtakes what the captain considers to be a pirate vessel, he captures it and seizes a treasure of gold coins. Then one of the sailors discovers a manifest or registry slip proving that the vessel was an American trading sloop from the port of Biloxi, which at that time was part of west Florida. After the captured sloop is wrecked in a

storm that separates the three men in it from the crew on the *Glimpse*, the wrecked seamen carry some of the gold coins with them when they swim ashore. They live among friendly Indians, and the two younger men take native women as wives. The older man dies of tropical fever, and the two young sailors finish the boat they had all begun together; then they sail to New Orleans.

In the meantime, the crewmen on the *Glimpse* have visited New Orleans, leaving behind them the sailor who had discovered the registry paper on the sloop. He is Jeremiah Disney, son of the Puritan minister at Chog's Cove. The temptations of New Orleans prove too much for him, and he becomes a drunken wastrel. When the two sailors from the sloop arrive in the city, he tries to blackmail them, accusing the men of piracy. In retaliation, they destroy his evidence, the manifest from the captured vessel. Finally, all the survivors of the voyage reassemble in Chog's Cove where the last act of drama occurs.

Jeremiah, tortured by conscience and his thirst for drink, tries to blackmail the captain. He threatens to ruin the other members of the crew and to disgrace the memory of those who have been lost. Caught in a fight between the master gunner and the gunner's drunken father, the guilt-ridden man runs across a marshy field into a pool and is drowned. He carries with him the secret of pirate gold; but the other seamen and the captain still possess their unlawful shares and remain secure in the esteem of their neighbors in Chog's Cove.

*Long Pennant* should have been La Farge's greatest work: his writing skill was mature; he was presenting character types which gave New England its distinctive culture—the Honorable Jonas Eliot Dodge, sea captain and also leader of the Federalist party; John Disney, widower and thrifty landowner, the first mate on Captain Dodge's ship; Jeremiah Disney, his nephew, son of a clergyman and filled with the fear of hell and damnation; Ephriam Brown and Roger Hall, able seamen, who were expected to bring home their earnings or winnings and marry the girls they left behind them. Both of these young stalwarts made amorous detours in Mexico and New Orleans, and only one of them redeems his pledge. There are others on the voyage, and to all of them Chog's Cove is the center of the moral and physical universe. Their freebooting trip during the War of 1812 brought experiences that changed the course of their lives both during and after the trip.

La Farge introduces his novel with a quotation from the *Odyssey*: "It is a harsh land, yet it breeds good youths; but perhaps in every man's sight there is nothing better than his native land." Homer said this of Ithaca, the home of Odysseus, but La Farge has made the words apply to New England. His travelers wander during a war, rather than after, as did Homer's argonauts; they are carried by storms to Lotus Land, as were the followers of Odysseus; and they return to faithful wives and sweethearts at Chog's Cove instead of Sparta. Greece and New England may not be exact counterparts, nor is Captain Dodge a replica of Odysseus; but the theme of a native land, including its way of life, is pursued by La Farge in much the manner of Homer in his Greek epic. However, the religious hysteria of Jeremiah Disney mars an otherwise convincing portrayal of character, and the picture of New Orleans becomes almost offensively lurid. The author's syntax at times is complex, and his diction is overloaded with nautical terms. Perhaps these drawbacks are some of the reasons *Long Pennant* was not a success.[12]

## IV   The Enemy Gods

Eight years separate *Laughing Boy* from *The Enemy Gods*, and there are two La Farges involved in the writing of these novels. The first is the youthful explorer, living in an exotic, mystical culture, in which men believed that they had been produced by the earth and the sky, that celestial deities still encircled all living things with influences that could be invoked by poetry, song, dance, and symbols. This protective medicine, aided by herbs, fetiches, plumes, and pollens, controlled all good and evil powers. The man who wrote *Laughing Boy* saw the Navajos as untouched by outside influences, living in an environment of primitive beauty and power. The author of *The Enemy Gods* had become more realistic about the Navajos as they were surrounded by government agencies, such as the Departments of Indian Affairs and of Public Health, the Forestry Service, the Reclamation Service, even the Post Office. Laughing Boy escaped from the boarding school and the missionaries who tried to "Americanize" Myron Begay, the young Navajo in *The Enemy Gods*. Myron may have had more of the author in his character, because, as he grew to manhood, he faced a choice between an old familiar way and one that was new; moreover, he tried to keep what he could of both, as did Oliver La Farge.

In commenting upon his second long narrative about the Navajos,

the author writes: "I think *The Enemy Gods* is my first non-escape writing though the critics do not agree with me."[13] Because editors expected him to write another romantic story, their attitude annoyed him. Furthermore, the attitude of the public was the same. When La Farge gave a lecture, members of the audience would come forward to say, "Oh, Mr. La Farge, I did so love your *Laughing Boy*! When are you going to give us another book?" He could scarcely reply, "I've written two since *Laughing Boy*, and you haven't read either one." *The Enemy Gods* does differ from *Laughing Boy* in its more realistic plot and events. The story proper begins in a government boarding school where a six-year-old Navajo boy has just been enrolled for his first year. His hair has been cut; he has been stripped, washed, deloused, and given new clothes—shocking experiences for a child who believed that long hair was sacred and who had never worn hard, heavy shoes. His father is dead, and his mother has remarried. A Protestant missionary befriends the boy; as the story develops, he becomes like a foster father since the boy spends his summers with the man and his wife. The rival to the Christians is Shooting Singer, the boy's uncle, who is a Navajo medicine man. There are no fewer Indian rituals in *The Enemy Gods*; and at crucial moments, as in *Laughing Boy*, their meaning turns the scales in favor of the hero's Navajo inheritance. The plot of La Farge's second novel covers a period of twenty-two years; the plot of his first was ended in one year and a half. The roots of Navajo traditions are more fully explored in *The Enemy Gods*.

Myron Begay does not wish to return to his home because he fears his stepfather. However, he is drawn to his medicine-man uncle; and, when the new Indian commissioner orders that boarding-school Indians spend more time with their own people, Myron returns to his home at Yellow Earth. Since his mother has moved elsewhere, he stays with his uncle and aunt. Ten years have passed before this visit, and Myron is now sixteen years old, the age of manhood for a Navajo boy. He is neither Navajo nor white in his way of life, neither savage nor civilized. On this trip, he attends a Mountain Chant, but he does not participate except to join in the singing. None of the Navajo girls selects him for a partner when the circle is formed for the Squaw Dance. Nevertheless, he does meet a girl from another government school, and he talks with her. When he learns that she is a Christian, he carries away thoughts that she might make him a good wife.

His uncle, the medicine man, tells him that the Navajos can only stand out as a people by retaining their own customs. They may adopt the clothing of the white people and their tools, but they cannot become white in thought or feeling. When Myron starts back to his school, the way is blocked by a flooded arroyo, and he stops at a hogan that seems to be abandoned. When he enters, he sees a fire under the smoke hole. A girl confronts him and tells him not to enter but when he offers her his rifle as a defense she accepts the gun with amusement and invites him to bring his saddle to shelter in the hogan.

This girl is Juniper, whose ceremonial name is "War Encircling." She has been married to a Navajo wastrel named Singing Gambler, who spends more time away from her hogan than he does in it. She gives herself to Myron; and, by this act, she becomes a center in his life that lasts through the years in which he attends the Santa Fe Indian School and plans to become a Protestant minister. La Farge is able to discuss all the problems of the Navajo people through Myron, who becomes the spokesman for programs being planned by the Association on American Indian Affairs of which La Farge was the president. Expanding the book to make *The Enemy Gods* a more comprehensive study of the Navajos increased its length, but the added material diffused the romance and substituted the problems Myron has in choosing between a Christian girl for his wife and an Indian woman who has not been given missionary training. The situation reverses, therefore, the relationship in *Laughing Boy*: the hero, rather than the heroine, chooses to abandon the white man's society, where he has lived for a good many years. *The Enemy Gods* is a more complete picture of the modern-day Navajos and is a more important work than *Laughing Boy*, but it lacks the popular appeal of the first novel.

## V    The Copper Pot *and* Cochise of Arizona

The neighborhood of the author's apartment and his friends in New Orleans are given fictional dressing in his novelette *No More Bohemia*, published in 1935 and revised as *The Copper Pot* in 1942. The essential theme in both plots is the conflict within the central figure, an artist, that is produced by his life in the French Quarter of the city and by the strict code of his upbringing in Rhode Island. Since this artist comes from La Farge's home state and has graduated from Harvard, the reader finds difficulty in not identifying

Tom Hartshorn in *The Copper Pot* with the author. Both also grew up in a Puritan environment, and the tenth chapter of La Farge's personal narrative *Raw Material* recounts episodes like those in the novel. A subtitle of the novel could have been "A Yankee in Search of Himself."

Tom Hartshorn, the Yankee in question, is a "remittance man from Chog's Cove, Rhode Island, the same port from which the sailors in *Long Pennant* had sailed more than one hundred years earlier. Tom's Uncle Standish and Aunt Martha pay his expenses while he paints and makes prints, earning an extra pittance by teaching a class at the Art Institute. To him, New Orleans has meant freedom of soul; and he expects to paint as he could never have painted in Chog's Cove. In a Bohemian society he meets a beautiful woman named Frances Warren, who has come from New York to write advertising for a New Orleans newspaper. A contrast to Frances is Estelle Garney, daughter of a wealthy plantation owner, who had been a student in Tom's art class. When Hartshorn is hired to paint a mural for her father's hotel, they meet often. He proposes marriage because she offers security in an enclosed way of life. He must choose between the safety of Estelle's world and the uncertain prospects of earning a living in the French Quarter. He finds Frances Warren to be a congenial companion who knows many of his Bohemian friends. After an artists' ball, Frances returns with him to his apartment. Although he is engaged to Estelle Garney, he makes love to Frances, and she accepts him as a lover. When he goes to her apartment the next afternoon, she proposes that they pool their rent money and share an apartment. Tom is forced to tell of his engagement. She accuses him of deceiving her, and they part with a comment by Frances that, although his fiancée is very rich, the fact may not solve all his problems.

After leaving Frances, Tom realizes that he loves her. In despair, he writes to Estelle to cancel their engagement and then rushes out to find Frances, but she is not in her apartment. When he learns from her best friend that she has left New Orleans, he calls himself "a damn fool and a stinking worm," crying "I have thrown perfect happiness out of the hollow of my hands."[14]

The preliminary Note to *The Copper Pot* is a rather elaborate effort to disassociate the book from identifying any real person. La Farge explains that the "true novelist" is not just a reporter; he creates characters by synthesizing many unrelated impressions

79

and by fusing them into imaginary beings. He admits that this creative freedom can make use of traits which resemble someone the author may know, but these resemblances are accidental, not intentional. Such comments, however, encourage readers to look for passages in the book which seem to reflect the author's personal experience.

The title of the novel is suggested by a huge metal container which was filled with bottles of various hues. It stood in the gallery of a boarding house next to Tom Hartshorn's studio; he painted it as a picture of serene beauty in the midst of mops, washtubs, and drying laundry. Tom feels that the scene arranges itself as he calculates the colors he will use and the position from which he will begin to paint. This is the attitude of a man controlled to a degree by his surroundings, playing his part in selecting what to see but limited by what is there.

La Farge wrote one more long narrative called *Cochise of Arizona,* which was completed eleven years after his last novel. Cochise, the Apache chieftain who was provoked by false charges into twelve years of warfare against American settlers, was finally persuaded to sign a truce when a stage-line operater named Jeffords rode into the Apache hideout and made a pact of blood brotherhood; he and Cochise cut their wrists and pressed them together, mixing blood with blood. Cochise kept the agreement he had made. La Farge omits the account of the blood pact, although in 1872 the governor of Arizona mentioned it and the newspapers carried articles about the ceremony at the time of Jefford's death. La Farge, as a scientist, may have omitted material that would have enlivened his story, because he felt that ethnological data was lacking. *Cochise of Arizona* is classified as a juvenile since neither in length nor in scope does it match the complex prose narratives which preceded it. [15]

## VI  *New Worlds in the Novels*

While writing his novels, La Farge never abandoned his viewpoint as an ethnologist. He was always examining old societies or the society in which he lived to discover what people sought in life in order to solve their problems with plans that were most successful. Like a horticulturist, who cross-pollinates or grafts, he made both past and present his laboratories. New worlds emerge for each of the fictitious heroes in his books, but these worlds are made

from fragments of societies that have been destroyed or societies that are rebuilding to avoid destruction.

The central figure in every novel is masculine: Sings Before Spears in *Laughing Boy*; Esteban Perez y Bagil in *Sparks Fly Upward*; Jeremiah or, perhaps, Roger Hall in *Long Pennant*; Seeing Warrior (Myron Begay) in *The Enemy Gods*; and Tom Hartshorn in *The Copper Pot*. Each of them has lived in what could be considered a closed society, and each is forced by circumstances to move into a more open world. The two Navajos find themselves moving across the boundaries of a ritualistic, clan-dominated pastoral environment into a free-moving, semi-industrial order in which the individual seeks his own security in a dollar-scaled economy. Esteban Perez moves from the artificial social status he had acquired into the middle group which presumably will merge the Indian and the Spanish social extremes into a classless society no longer dominated by hierarchies in church and state.

Finding a single figure so central to *Long Pennant* is not easy, for the plot shifts the interest from character to character. However, the fortunes of all depend upon Jeremiah Disney, the Puritan from Chog's Cove, who tries to force his life-corroding moral strictures upon the world outside. When he fails, the small circle he had infected is purified. His departure, then, contributed to a better point of view in his own community. In *The Copper Pot*, the experiences of Tom Hartshorn clearly contrast two regional environments, the northeast seaboard and the southern Gulf Coast. The reader will conclude that Tom profited in his early life from the discipline of one and in later life from the courtesy of the other. The best of both possible environments seems to wait for him to develop a personal maturity.

Of the women characters in the novels, only two are outstanding: Slim Girl in *Laughing Boy* and Frances Warren in *The Copper Pot*. Slim Girl was destroyed by contacts with a number of selfish and cruel men;yet she found salvation in one man who was devoted and considerate. What seems to be inconsistent in her motivation results from the insecurity in her youth as an orphan; from her seduction by an American cowboy; from her rejection by the family that had given her a home; from her association with prostitutes who befriended her; and from the alliance with the rancher whose money she continued to accept after her marriage to Laughing Boy. She justified herself with her pretext of revenge upon white Americans,

but this rationalization did not remove the conflict between two courses before her—Indian culture and white civilization. Her death foretells the social as well as the personal struggle facing her people.

Frances Warren is more a symbol than the cause of the conflict in *The Copper Pot*. Tom Hartshorn is already trying to move from the old world of his youth into a new one. When he meets Frances, he finds that she combines the outlook of his past with her own creative mind and personality; but his limitations prevent him from making a decisive choice, and the new horizon does not appear for him until she has gone. In *Sparks Fly Upward*, Doña Favia, who lives in the world of the old social order, is above the hero in both rank and wealth. She is the victim of change when Esteban Perez turns to the Indian woman, Marta Checheb, who represents the coming new society in the land of Alturas.

The girl Juniper is also a symbol rather than a cause for the plot to develop in *The Enemy Gods*, for Myron Begay chooses her when he decides to live as a Navajo. His program is to bring the worlds of the Navajo and the white man together; but, since the Navajo world will be the base of operations, Juniper will anchor him there. In *Long Pennant*, the women play no significant role unless they are regarded as part of the terrestrial facade behind the men. They are static rather than dynamic figures. Hope Langdon and the other sweethearts call the men back from the women in the Caribbean and New Orleans, but the men return to their native Rhode Island as much from duty as from desire. Thus, the viewer of the worlds in the La Farge novels recognizes the rejected foreign sirens, the steadfast native homemakers, the courageous adventurers crossing from old situations into new, and the women secure between old and new. Women become havens for men whose fortunes are in transition, and they are sometimes sacrificed when they seem nonessential. La Farge may be said to have found a mystique for the role of women in this process of mediating the destructive and regressive influences of men. His creative drive, whether in fiction or in life, tried to narrow the swing of social changes so that they touched the edges of the old and moved toward the new without a breakdown or uncontrollable shift of course.

In constructing plots for his novels, La Farge showed unusual skill. The sequence of events or plot continuity is arranged according to three patterns: linear, collateral, or cyclical. A linear plot is a story in which the life of the central figure is presented chronolog-

ically, and conflicts occur for him in a continuous time sequence. The first two novels he wrote fit into this category, although *Laughing Boy* is condensed into an interval of less than two years and *Sparks Fly Upward* requires twenty-four years for the story to unfold. Yet both novels proceed without shifts in the direction line for the heroes. *Long Pennant* is quite different in the arrangement of events, for its plot can be described as both collateral and cyclical. There are three separate strands of narrative, which are told concurrently but also with flashbacks of memory by individual characters. The central strand concerns the career of Captain Dodge and the main crew of the *Glimpse*; the second thread deals with the sailors who were shipwrecked and return to New England via the coast of Mexico and New Orleans; the third narrative concerns Jeremiah Disney, who learns the secret of the captured sloop and uses it for purposes of blackmail. These stories are told separately and are unified at the end when the men are released from fear by the death of Jeremiah. As previously stated, La Farge modeled his plot on Homer's *Odyssey*, which has one story for the hero, Odysseus; another for the hero's wife, Penelope; and a third for their son, Telemachus. The stories are collateral until Odysseus begins to relate adventures in his past; the narrative then becomes cyclical as flashbacks occur to recall previous experiences. The sailors in *Long Pennant* have similar moments of reminiscence during their long voyage.

La Farge's fourth novel, *The Enemy Gods*, combines elements of both linear and collateral plotting. The story of the central character, Myron Begay, proceeds from the day he begins his education in a government boarding school and continues to the moment he leaves high school without finishing his studies for a diploma. In the Prologue to the book, the Indian War Gods hold a dialogue. They are called the Twins or Slayers of Enemy Gods, and they act as protectors of the Navajos. As they rise and stand above the sky, they watch Myron and then say: "Let us pay attention not only to the Navajos but beyond them, to the sources of all that afflicts them." The Prologue states that they watch for a brief hour, but it was the entire span of sixteen years in Myron's life. Christian and Navajo localities provide centers of action to make a collateral plot in the boy's life. He also moves in a marginal world between the two earth centers, a kind of nonworld with the gods on the mountains.

In *The Copper Pot*, the last novel La Farge wrote, he devised what could be described as a "compressed linear" plot; for it covers events in one place, the neighborhood of New Orleans, within a period of two years. The central figure in the novel moves in a group of a dozen characters, each with claims upon his time and interest; but the plot is so well organized that each contributes in some way to the psychological involvement in which Tom Hartshorn, the hero, finds himself.

Mastery of time, place, and action are essential to the construction of a lengthy plot. La Farge exhibited craftmanship in a flexible way as he adjusted different materials in each of the five novels. In all of them, these skills served his primary purpose, which was to present a new outlook on older societies, protraying the flaws which brought grief rather than fulfillment to both individuals and communities.

# Participant and Observer:
# Short Stories

C ONSUELO La Farge describes how methodical her husband was about his working hours and how careful he was to find the right word and to check the exact punctuation marks. La Farge wrote and revised the short stories at his typewriter, bringing the material in to read to Consuelo and then correcting pages as he read them, often changing a word that had been used too many times or rearranging the structure of a sentence. Consuelo reports that she used to raise objections when the meaning was not clear. He wrote the novels in long hand, using an orange-colored paper which was ordered especially for this work. It was of tinted litho-stock, strong enough to take erasures and bright enough to serve as a background for either pencil or ink marks.

He gave two days of every week to the association of which he was president, and then he kept four days for writing. He made use of the extra bedroom as his study before John Pendaries was born; after that event, he worked in the living room or, when the addition to the front of the house was finished, in the office. Working faithfully in the morning from nine to twelve, he took a twenty-minute siesta after lunch before starting the afternoon session from two to five. Sometimes the length of the afternoon working period depended upon how successful the writing had been in the morning or upon how tired he had become. In an interview that he gave to a reporter in 1951, La Farge described himself as "the kind of a writer who interrupts his work by pacing the floor, emptying ash trays, straightening pictures on the wall or just plain jumping up and down." He added that observers would think his behavior hopelessly idiotic. He also said that he could not work with anyone else in the room. [1]

As both critic and creative writer, La Farge felt an obligation to judge the writing of others, knowing that in due time judgment

would also be passed by others upon his own work. In one of the weekly newspaper columns he wrote during March, 1952, he refers to a British commentator who divided American authors into literary schools called "the participants" and "the observers." This critic considered Hemingway and Dreiser to be participants; Truman Capote and Tennessee Williams, observers. To the British critic, participants identified to a greater degree with their fictional characters than did the observers. In some cases, identification may happen as the author appears to tell the story himself, thus becoming a member of the cast. However, the reader can sometimes feel the identification in disguised ways, as when the author uses sympathetic words to project an attitude discoverable in his own personality or offers praise through his commentary to a vocation or pastime which he actually has experienced.

This capacity for participation is notable in many of the La Farge stories. The transfer from author to character is never exactly revealed. No reader has to see the countenance of Oliver peering through the eyes of young Lansing at Saint Peter's School when he becomes the victim of a bully in the story called "By the Boys Themselves," and La Farge need not be the anthropologist Hendricks in the story "The Ancient Strength." Yet something in each of these characters can be associated with a past experience of the writer. They are packaged fragments of his own life, but they are so artistically presented that they become objective insights to someone else's life, and the reader is able to make them part of his own.

## I  *Participant and Observer*

Artfully shaped stories are always designed from factual materials. They are never nature undirected even in the stream-of-consciousness type of revelation, but there is an artistry, or contrivance, in every one of them if they are to bring meaning and pleasure to a reader. An author recognizes the elements which his story must have: first, a recognizable setting for characters portrayed in satisfaction or dissatisfaction with things as they are or have been; second, an event or a discovery of knowledge which brings a change to this situation; third, a conflict between the central character and the forces opposing him; and fourth, the resolution of conflict in triumph or defeat for this central character. Two short stories of contrasting type illustrate the author's share as participant or as observer.

In the first story, Sherwood Anderson's "I Want to Know Why," the narrator is a fifteen-year-old boy who lives in a Kentucky town and has grown up around thoroughbred horses. He has admiration for their courage, cleanliness, and decency. These human traits fit the racehorses he admires. When one of the horses is guided to victory by a trainer whom the boy also admires, his world of human as well as animal qualities becomes perfected. After the successful race to victory, the boy follows the trainer to a house of pleasure, where he sees the man in the company of women the lad believes to be bad. As the boy watches the trainer gazing at one of these women in the same way he had gazed at the beautiful horse that had made the day radiant with glory, his love for the man turns to hate. He wants to know why good and evil can exist at the same time in the one person he most admired. This outline of a plot cannot bring the warmth of participation which the writer seems to share with the boy in Anderson's story. The writer succeeds in involving the reader in the story—bringing him to the height of the lad's joy at the triumph of horse and trainer and then in reversing his mood to dismay and bewilderment with the youth's discovery of the trainer's imperfection.

A short story by Katherine Mansfield illustrates the more impersonal technique maintained by the observer. Here the reader's interest is equally engrossed, but the author seems less involved. In her story, "The Fly," Miss Mansfield first introduces an old man who has retired from his business and who trundles into the city on occasions to visit with his former business associates. On the day of the story, he is sitting in the office of a man who is simply called the "boss." The boss is still active, and he glows with the satisfaction of pointing to new furnishings and improvements in his office. The old visitor says that his daughters have been to their brother's grave in a military cemetery in France. They also reported finding the grave of the boss's son nearby. All the graves were beautifully cared for, and the old man asks the boss if he has ever gone to see his son's burial place. The answer is negative.

After the visitor has departed, the boss instructs his secretary to admit no one for half an hour. He then covers his face with his hands while he remembers the son and the plans he had made for him in the business, the emptiness of life after the young man's death, and the six years of grief that had followed. Today, he is puzzled that the loss seems less severe. He looks at the boy's pho-

tograph, but he is not moved as he had always been. At that moment, a fly falls into the inkpot. As it slides backward on the glass, the boss lifts it with a pen and drops the sodden body on a piece of blotting paper. Then he watches while the fly cleans its wings, one after the other, stretching each preparatory to flight. The boss is absorbed in the struggle to survive. Desiring to test the fly further, he drops a great blob of ink upon the body before the wings can spread. The insect is stunned, but it painfully pulls forward on the blotter and begins to scrape again, cleaning the legs and wings as before. The boss refills his pen and drops a second blob of ink; then, after the fly resumes the cleaning process, he drops a third. With this blow, the motion of the fly stops. The struggle is over. The boss pushes the body to stir it to life, but the fly is limp. A wave of sorrow crosses the boss's mind. He cannot recall what he was thinking about before he began to watch the fly. There is only a blank as he calls for a secretary to come and clean his desk.

The artistry of Mansfield matches that of Anderson; yet the techniques of the two writers are very different. The point of view of one is involvement; of the other, observation. The observation is so close that not a twitch of a muscle escapes notice. Both methods supply characters with thoughts immediate to the action, and neither the subjectivity of one nor the objectivity of the other can be considered superior as an approach to narrative writing. Oliver La Farge makes use of both points of view, although he seems more often to be the participant in his insight than the observer.

## II  *La Farge as Participant*

Several of his stories may be cited as illustrating the participant approach to narrative subject matter. First, in the story "North is Black," the opening line reads: "It is true that we say that North is black and cold and bad because of the stories of our old men, but those are good stories." The "we" in the text is a plural for the narrator, who speaks as a member of the Navajo tribe and of the cast in the story. He says that he is old and that his name is North Wanderer. He asks for coffee and then begins a tale about his life. With this opening, North Wanderer is addressing an audience of which the reader could be one. The reader, like the narrator, is one of the circle of those listening to North Wanderer's story about his love for a white woman and of how he discovered that he could not join her in a world where both would be happy. The device is as old as story-

telling, where the bard or tribal narrator looks backward to experiences he has known. La Farge draws upon his anthropology to
describe how North Wanderer studied with the medicine man called
Mountain Singer. The visits La Farge made to Navajoland provide
details for his hero's visit to the North and the stay at the ranch of
the American woman, followed by his character's return to the reservation after learning how wide the gap between red man and
white could be. Participation by the writer depends upon his background of knowledge as well as upon the device which seems to
make him enter the story as narrator with the chief character.

Six years after La Farge wrote "North Is Black," a story about
an Indian among white people, he produced one about white people
among Indians, "The Women at Yellow Wells." The opening line
reads: "She pushed aside the tablet and laid down her pencil." The
woman is Jane, wife of a trader on an Indian reservation; her home
is at a trading post called Yellow Wells. In the next few lines, the
reader joins Navajo men lounging in the store and Indian women
helping the wife to close the trading post for the night. The reader
thinks Jane's thoughts as she thinks them, and he comes to the same
conclusion she does about the dangers while her husband is away.
Her tensions are those of the reader, who shares her point of view.
When her husband returns, the reader relaxes with Jane; both have
come safely through a night of threatened danger. In "North Is
Black," Northern Stranger's viewpoint was his as an individual,
because he referred to himself during the story. In "The Women
at Yellow Wells," Jane becomes the reader's alter ego because the
reader substitutes his position for hers in the story. La Farge has
persuaded him to do so.[2]

Other stories by La Farge which demonstrate the quality of participation are "First Day," written in 1938, and "Old Century's
River," which appeared in 1950. The first is about a boy's school
very similar to Groton, the school the author attended. The boy
Weatherbee is small as Oliver was; he loved music as Oliver did;
he experienced bullies; and he was lonely—all characteristics or
experiences confessed by Oliver in *Raw Material*. There are five
stories about this imaginary Saint Peter's School which are listed
in La Farge's bibliography.[3] Five more such stories are to be found
among his unpublished manuscripts, including two typewritten
pages giving a list of characters designed for the faculty and student body. Young Weatherbee appears in all the published stories.

He is called by the nickname "Inky" in "The Touch of Greatness," after he cleaned up the ink spots in an autograph book for the school hero to sign. As has been previously pointed out, this was La Farge's own boyhood nickname.

### III   *Old Century's River*

The setting for "Old Century's River" could be one of the jungles explored by La Farge and Blom when they were in southern Mexico making notes for *Tribes and Temples*. The iguanas, jaguars, snakes, and insects which shared the solitude of William Tecumseh Carpenter, are similar to those encountered by La Farge as a young anthropologist early in his professional career. Carpenter, the American engineer, was called "Old Century" because, as a scout for an oil company, he told everyone he met that he had come to the river country "at the turn of the century, when I was a young sprout." That was fifty years ago, he reminisces with the reader. It is not necessary to push the case for La Farge as participant to argue that he was ever in pain as Old Century was on the banks of a river or that his only friends had been two whiskey bottles like those which consoled Carpenter after the plane crashed in the forest. The two young men Carpenter offered to guide on a treasure hunt abandoned him, and the liquor bottles were all he could find after they left for help. Old Century knew they never would escape the jungle. For three weeks he had suffered there. His mind slips back into memories of friends and sweethearts, the wonderful visits to Mexico City, and the fearful encounter with bandits who carried off the native girl with whom he had lived. Visions pass through his fantasy while the poisonous pain creeps from his battered leg toward his heart.

Old Century holds the whiskey and measures the line of shadow between himself and the river bank. It seems that there is some association between the level in the bottle and the moving line of moonlight around him. What was left to him but whiskey and the river? They alone fought against the gangrenous death gripping his leg. He takes a piece of newspaper and makes a cigarette from the butts that remain. As the smoke eddies into the mist, he lets himself down into the water, welcoming the chill because it eases his pain. The crutches float away, and he takes a long last pull at the bottle. His hand falls, dropping the flask into the water with a faint gurgle. Slowly he follows; with eyes closed, he slips gently

Participant and Observer: Short Stories

into the stream where he drifts without motion of his own.[4]

In "The Bright Faces," the boy and the girl are about the ages of the two La Farge children at that time. They have been sent to visit with their father, who has just returned from military service and is divorced from their mother. When he meets them at a hotel, he hopes that they will come home with him and share his vacation. He last saw them four years ago. (La Farge was in the Air Transport Command for four years.) Now he expects to have them for a while as his own. When he mentions his plan, the boy (who is older) explains that both of them are booked for the summer and cannot change their arrangememts. The father, angered, threatens to exercise his legal rights to take them with him. Then he notices their determined faces, and he realizes that he has lost and that the mother has won. The story could be referred to the life of the author, and a caption could be applied from a cinema script: "This story is true. Only the names and places have been changed to protect the innocent."

## IV  Patterns of Story Writing

Whatever an author's narrative point of view, a short story can develop as action only by discord or struggle in a background where the characters seek an outcome favorable to their welfare. Two patterns of development emerge to solve such struggles: one is the reversal of a physical situation for the hero or heroine; the other, a change in the psychological relationship they have to themselves and to others. The second type of change comes from discovery and recognition of facts which have been concealed. This adjustment is an emotional one rather than a change in prosperity or some other form of outward profit. In Sherwood Anderson's story "I Want to Know Why," the boy did not experience any loss of physical well-being when he learned of the trainer's weakness; but when he learned an unpleasant truth, the discovery changed him from happiness to misery. Many of La Farge's short stories, especially those written in later life, are built upon the discovery- or recognition-type of plot. In some of his stories, both physical and intellectual changes occur. The hero not only improves his lot by material gain, but also changes his attitude by learning new facts about himself.

The chart below indicates that, until 1957, La Farge's plot types are almost equally balanced between these two schemes, with about

one-third of them combining the two reversals; but all the stories written after 1957 make use of recognition shifts. Of the total of forty plots, slightly more than half depend upon reversals by recognition.

## CHART OF STORY PLOTS

|  | Reversal of Physical Situation | Change in Both Situation and Facts | Recognition of Hidden Facts |
|---|---|---|---|
| *All the Young Men* (1935) | 5 | 2 | 5 |
| *A Pause in the Desert* (1957) | 6 | 5 | 5 |
| *The Door in the Wall* (1965) | 0 | 0 | 12 |

### V  *Physical and Recognition Plots*

A brief sketch of several plots found in stories from these collections of short stories clarifies the distinction between a plot of physical reversal and one of recognition of concealed facts. In 1950, La Farge constructed a plot for a story called "La Spécialté de M. Duclos." Duclos, a French chef, practices his cooking art in Connecticut, where he operates his own restaurant. In pursuit of this vocation he has stabbed one of his patrons to death. After he escapes to France, the American authorities try to extradite him to the United States for trial. The judge at the hearing is president of the Gastronomic Society of Legal Advocates, and the counselor for the defense is a gourmet as well as a brilliant lawyer. He begins his defense by telling about the eating habits of Americans, especially those who live in Connecticut and work in the adjoining metropolis of New York City. Few of them know how to cook, he announces; fewer still can distinguish between the wines of California and of France. Until this point, those in the courtroom, as well as those on the bench, have displayed little interest in the fate of M. Duclos. Now their attention grows as the advocate stresses the pride this Frenchman had in his cooking as he approached the moment of his crime.

While experimenting in the preparation of a white sauce, M. Duclos had discovered an amazing variation upon one of the simplest elements of all cookery. He realized that this preparation might make him famous and that he could transfer it to France where it would draw Americans and help his countrymen win prosperity under the Marshall Plan. To advertise the sauce, he invited a select group of patrons to dinner. When all of them exclaimed over the dressing and then asked for the recipe, Duclos only smiled; but, upon returning to the kitchen, one of the guests followed him. Before Duclos could stop the intruder, Duclos saw him checking ingredients on the shelf where the sauce had been prepared. Shaken by the experience, the chef returned to the table where he heard the man say to his neighbor: "Come to dinner next Wednesday, old boy" and then heard him name three of the ingredients used in the secret recipe. When M. Duclos thought of the peril to his sauce and to his reputation as a chef, he suddenly seized a carving knife and stabbed his guest to death as an enemy of France and her culinary genius.

In order to dramatize the situation in the courtroom, a table is wheeled in, and on it are the cooking equipment and the ingredients he had used. He prepares the sauce; the judges taste it; and the effect is electrical: Duclos is freed by a unanimous decision of the judges. Their verdict is rendered on the basis that theft of the recipe was burglary, and that burglary could be resisted by force. The courtroom cheers; M. Duclos embraces his lawyer.

The next morning, the lawyer goes first to his office and then to his apartment. Arriving there, he immediately proceeds to the kitchen. In seclusion he tests the three secret ingredients he had seen mixed by M. Duclos in the courtroom, but he does not know the exact amounts of each. When the sauce is not right, he sighs and starts again. Absorbed in his problem, he does not notice that someone has entered the apartment. Turning, he sees Duclos, who should have already boarded the train for his home in the countryside. "You experiment, Monsieur l'Advocat?" asks Duclos, pointing to one of the ingredients. "No good cook would think I ever used that in a sauce. I had a phial of it along as a blind." Then he draws a knife, caressing it with the fingers of his left hand. "It is almost an exact duplicate of the fine knife with which I eliminated the American." As he stabs the lawyer, he knows that the judge who had freed him before will no doubt free him again.[5]

The plot of "La Spécialté de M. Duclos" depends upon a reversal of physical peril, but it also has the element of recognition as it repeats the original plot. The story could be said to have double reversals: the first, when Duclos was under threat for slaying the American; the second, when the threat is repeated for slaying the Frenchman. An earlier story, "Haunted Ground," also has multiple reversals and shifts in recognition. In this story, which won the O. Henry Short Story Prize for 1930, a boat is wrecked on the New England coast; and a young man finds himself on the beach looking toward a house long believed to stand on ghostly terrain. He knows that a dead girl lies in the home, the victim of a robber caught at his burglary.

The young man climbs the bluff; and, when no one answers, he enters and sees a coffin in the sitting room. Opposite the coffin the mother of the girl is resting on a chair. She speaks to him, but her voice has a vague quality. He hears a sound like heartbeats; they seem to come from outside or from within his ears. The mother speaks of the girl's fiancé, who had been lost in a wreck in the harbor. She believes that the two will be united after a funeral. The young man decides the mother is demented. He hears heartbeats again, along with footsteps, and thinks someone is pulling at his shoulder. When he passes this information along to the woman, she cries out that he must return to the beach. As he opens the door to her bedroom, he sees the mother's body lying on the bed, serene and pale in death. He dashes toward the door, brushing the girl's coffin as he tries to leave. Then he stops and sits down, saying, "Those heartbeats are very slow; they'll be over in a minute."

The shiftings in "Haunted Ground" occur on both physical and psychological levels. The reader is first on the beach with the young man gazing at the fragments of the boat. Then he is on the bluff with the shadow-image of the man, whose spirit remains with the body on the beach. Finally, he is at the threshold of the house where the spirit of the man is unable to return to its body. The reversals in the physical situation occur as the man dies on the beach. Shifts in recognition for both reader and the dying man occur as the man learns that he is changing from a physical being into a wraith or apparition, aware of other apparitions like himself who are in a state of transition between life and death. Even the dead fiancé is presented as waiting at the fringe of consciousness for his bride-to-be. The story is not long, nor is it fully developed; but the reality

or unreality of the entire framework illustrates the sweep of La Farge's imagination, as well as resourcefulness in plot development on two levels.[6]

All of the Talvert University stories are of the recognition pattern. They number eight narrative, portraitlike sketches of anthropologists or ethnologists who come to realize their various stages of success or frustration. In "Independent Research," an anthropologist who has been too long among the natives in Central America discovers that his failure to publish has permanently exiled him to a village of thatched huts where he has a native wife and child. In the story "The Resting Place," physical change does occur; but it is the fulfillment of the process of recognition which comes first and is the true plot break. An old veteran of archaeological research has been suspected of removing ceremonial objects, such as feathers, shells, and turquoise, from a museum case. When he joins a party to excavate a ruin near the Four Corners area in Arizona, a younger scientist is instructed to keep track of him. The older man finds an excuse to visit another "dig" where he had conducted research early in his career; indeed, his custom has been to visit the place every year.

Arriving late in the afternoon, he deposits his bedroll and his food; then he cuts a supply of firewood. Taking a package wrapped in an old piece of buckskin, he climbs to the ruin to visit a kiva where he had worked long ago. Under a rock he finds a crude stone pipe which he fills with tobacco, makes curious gestures as he lights it, and then puffs smoke in the six directions. He climbs out of the kiva, opens the buckskin package, and extracts ancient beads of turquoise, pieces of white and red shell, black stone, feathers of eagle down, and corn pollen. When he speaks to someone sitting opposite him, the voice answers, thanking him for the offerings he has brought. The voice then offers to guide him to the Spirit World of the Ancients; it promises the old archaeologist that, free of his rheumatic bones, he will dance with the god-spirits there. The voice urges his friend to lie down in the crevice near the ruin and to make up his mind. There the searchers find him several days later. He had joined the kachinas, spirit deities, of the Indian world, who had become more real to him than the spirits of his own people.[8]

The recognition plot, in general, depends upon the elements of character rather than upon dramatic turns of events. In the hands of a skillful artist, the portrait drawn is memorable; the experience

recorded is significant; the fragment of life is part of a larger whole which it illuminates. The stories of Oliver La Farge tell what people think and feel as well as what they do. The narratives offer a wide range of characters and themes. Each of them extends the imagination of a reader and enriches his total experience.

# Part III

# SCIENTIST AND HISTORIAN

The world needs now, not the mere knowledge of science, but the way of thought and the discipline.

. . . the vision of ancient, far-off, tremendous happenings, of the march of primitive, great, bearded men out of Asia, the wagons and the cattle in motion as whole nations marched slowly, blindly to new lands, of wars and migrations, tide on tide.

Helping to restore a world in which free writing can exist strikes me as one of a writer's prime functions. I never believed much in the ivory tower.

If I had to pick out the occupational groups from which I receive the most today, I should say with a good deal of certainty that they were fellow-artists, newspapermen, and those scientists who have retained some realism and sense of humor.

—From *Raw Material*
(Used with permission)

# Animated Antiquity:
# Early Scientific Writings

**I** LIVED FOR A MONTH with the letter *k*," writes La Farge, as he describes the painstaking care with which a linguist pursues the sound shifts from one dialect of a language to another. He recognizes that what seems to be an insignificant item in linguistic geography could lead to historical information about the migration of Indian people across southern Mexico and Central America. He is also pointing out how thankless such a search can be sometimes if it turns out to be wasted effort. La Farge was the linguist on the First Tulane Expedition to Middle America in 1925, and his specific reporting in the book *Tribes and Temples* is found in six of the ten appendices to the text. These are linguistic reports, and they are signed "By Oliver La Farge." They deal with word lists, grammar, and specimen texts in Mayan, accompanied by Spanish and English equivalents. During these years of research, he found in Guatemala a manuscript which contained a vocabulary and grammar of one of the extinct Mayan languages, and he published material which established contacts for him with scholars in both Spain and Germany.[1]

## I  Tribes and Temples

Professor Blom, who was in charge of the expedition, was an artist as well as a scientist. He drew designs of the Mayan hieroglyphs and reconstructions of the temples which were based on scientific data. Blom's occasional descriptions of La Farge are line drawings, quick-penciled outlines of his actions: "Down on the eastern side of the pyramid, where the stairway leading up from the Plaza to the doors of the Temple used to be, La Farge found a fragment of a large stucco head modeled on a core of burnt brick" (I,iii). "While the boys unloaded the pack animals, La Farge took a nap, squatting

on the points of his spurs" (I,166). "La Farge discovered the altar
which lay face down" (I,215). "As we rode into the village, La
Farge discovered a stone block, carved with hieroglyphs, set in the
pavement of the sidewalk, an excellent reception for archaeologists"
(II, 247). "On top of the main mound, La Farge discovered a hole
in the ground, a thing an archaeologist cannot find without having
to see what is inside" (I, 223). After Oliver discovered the hole,
his companion let a candle down on a stick; and the light revealed
a chamber of the pyramid where beautiful jars stood in a row,
arranged as urns around the skeleton of a man. One of the teeth in
the skull had been inlaid with a black stone—ornamentation common to men of noble rank.

At other places in the story of geographical progress, Blom tells of
the thrill Oliver experienced when he first saw a cluster of Mayan
ruins—an entire city, with palaces, temples, and enclosed courts.
Blom's style is vivid as he praises the architectural achievements
of the Mayans. He compares their temples with those of ancient
Babylonia, Assyria, and Egypt. Some of his imaginative passages,
while picturing the building of one of the great pyramids, help the
reader to see slaves hauling a huge stone block by pulling at taut
vines until the block moves a few feet. Over in the main plaza of the
ruins, other workers are feeding limestone to a large kiln as men
carry buckets of lime, stones, and dirt to build the Sun Temple.
From the hill comes the song of the men at the quarries, cutting
tablets by the slow process of chipping stone against stone.[2] With
equal skill, Blom describes the palm-thatched huts where the work-
man lived, as did the men who were in the fields or the hunters
who provided food for the nobles and the townspeople.

Blom regrets that newspapers give much space to the sensational
aspects of archaeology but rarely report the drudgery connected
with working late hours over old maps, selecting the equipment for
life in dense forests or barren wastes, and surviving the dangers of
wild animals, snakes, and insects. La Farge was to make the same
comment twenty years later when he referred to some popular lecturers as the "hardship and danger boys" who exploited the ground
work of their predecessors in exploration and discovery; then they
exaggerated their own adventures with alligators, lions, jaguars,
and hostile natives. Such lecturers, he pointed out, write the travel
books and prepare the sound tracks for moving-picture cameras,
but they add nothing to the research which makes anthropology

a science.[3] The maps, drawings, tables, all the scientific data in the text and appendices, make *Tribes and Temples* a comprehensive presentation of both ancient and contemporary Mayans.

After collecting much ethnological information, Oliver had still failed to observe an Indian funeral; but this gap filled when the group stopped at a village where a man had been killed. He had been living with his sister as man and wife. Another Indian, who was married, desired her. The two men quarreled, and the brother knifed his rival, who then got a shotgun and killed his attacker. The survivor escaped; but, when he later returned for his own wife, he was captured. The family of the dead man held a wake and a funeral, both of which La Farge was permitted to attend. Frans Blom treated the wounds of the captured slayer, who was then turned over to the civil authorities for trial and probable hanging.

Although the field trip to Mexico was La Farge's first expedition with an investigator as experienced as Blom, it was the fourth summer he had spent exploring ruins of rare ethnological interest. Furthermore, all the Indians of the Americas—North, Central, and South—had much in common. All had a religion of the nature gods; their cultures were based on dance rituals and gifts propitiating the spirit world. Many of their handcrafts made use of the same materials and resembled one another. Their technology had grown out of the stone age, and their knowledge of metals was limited. Moreover, their great buildings extended north from Mexico to the massive structures of the early Pueblo Indians in New Mexico and Arizona. Even the star-lore had some things in common. Although the Navajo Indians never developed a calendar stone or left records in hieroglyphic carvings as did the Mayans, their sandpaintings tell of a great religious mythology based upon creation stories relating earth to sky and land to water. Before he was twenty-four years old, La Farge became immersed in the Indian world of this continent. Professor Tozzer of Harvard was the high priest of this anthropological awakening. Professor Blom of Tulane was the evangelist in the science of man who carried forward the development of La Farge in a professional career.

## II   The Year Bearer's People

The young ethnologist took another step forward when he and Douglas Byers published the material they had gathered on the Third Tulane Expedition. Their notebooks became *The Year Bear-*

*er's People*, which appeared in 1931. The book may have had less interest for the general reader than *Tribes and Temples* because it contained more of ethnology and less of archaeology. There is more glamor about uncovering monuments, finding statues or jewelry or fossil remains than about scientific description of calendar rites, agricultural practices, social organization, or even festivals. However, *The Year Bearer's People* devotes the last two chapters to archaeological discoveries and, as a whole, is a model of ethnological research, presenting the background for the Mayas in all southern Mexico, Yucatan, and Guatemala.

The title of the book stresses a system of measuring time which divided the solar (that is, the earth's) yearly rotation into eighteen months of twenty days each, leaving four or five days to honor lay priests called Name Bearers. There was one Name Bearer for each of the days remaining in the solar year, but their term of service was for only two hundred and sixty days, after which they were replaced by another group of Name Bearers. In some regions, these officials were treated as gods because they presided over the calendar and its record of natural phenomena, such as the name and significance assigned to each of the twenty days in the month. There was a day for the planting of grain and one for chile; some days favorable to fowls and those to animals; others, portending good health; and those guarding against ill will and slander. In fact, every aspect of nature and human life was covered by a kind of universal computer using these twenty designated name days, plus another cycle of day numbers from one to thirteen, which was counted within the twenty and either reinforced the day name or mitigated it. Both cycles operated within the two hundred and sixty days of each set of Name Bearers. Mayan forecasting can be compared to European and Asiatic astrology plus numerology, thereby showing the special role the Central American soothsayers had in the daily lives of the people.

When the Name Bearers retired, they were given a ceremonial feast called a "farewell to the village." A chicken or turkey was tied to a table used as an altar in a house for three days, during which period there could be no quarreling or drunkenness to disturb the atmosphere. On the night of the ceremony, the bird was decapitated, and the blood was burned on the altar. The chicken was then boiled with corn meal, and the family with a few friends partook of a ceremonial meal. When a group of religious officials met for such

a feast, they sacrificed the birds at wayside crosses and caught the blood on husks of corn which were burned before these symbols. Many of the crosses were fifty feet high; one rose to the height of seventy feet.[4]

Some scholars have argued that the Mayan cross was a design known in pre-Columbian times. Among Indian tribes, two crossed sticks indicated the four directions or the four winds, which may explain why the cross became adopted so rapidly after the introduction of Christianity in Central America. The Mayans looked upon their crosses as divinities, believing that they could see, think, hear, and even speak to those who could communicate with them. One of the soothsayers told Byers and La Farge that the crosses to which he appealed answered "yes" or "no" when he had inquired about the whereabouts of a lost mule. Finally, the cross near the mule, answered "yes," and the mule was found.[5] The crosses whether in country or town, were always decorated with flowers. No matter how scarred the woods became or how old the beams, they were never repaired, perhaps because the people regarded them as growing old like themselves. When the crosses at last fell, they were always replaced. Curiously, in view of their sacred character, crosses did not often appear in the native Mayan churches, either because there was rarely any room for them inside a building, or because the people preferred them in the open where the trees from which they were constructed once grew and where crosses always were put to use.

After the Spanish conquest in the sixteenth century, Mayan religion was an adaptation of pagan beliefs to Christianity. One illustration of this was the association of a *nagual* or companion spirit with the soul of any individual who happened to be born on a name day when that animal was mentioned or to be assigned by a shaman to an animal selected when the child was born. Often the animal as *nagual* was chosen to bring strength to a man and to help him to overcome his enemies. Another way for a *nagual* to become a part of a man's life was for the man to see such an animal in a dream, a theory which relates to some of the initiation rites to manhood adopted by southwestern and other Indian tribes in North America. Among the Mayans, men would shoot an animal known to be an enemy's *nagual* in hope that, by killing the beast, they would also harm the person who was a foe. A well-known Indian, whose *nagual* was a lion, once stopped at a ranch where the owner had just shot

a lion and hung it up. The Indian recognized the animal as his companion spirit, and he predicted that he, too, would die. Shortly afterwards, the Indian became sick; his prophecy of death came true.[6]

*The Year Bearer's People* is encyclopedic in its contents. Although somewhat shorter than *Tribes and Temples*, it covers both the ethnology and the languages of the area northwest of Huehuetanango, Guatemala. La Farge had previously studied the Mayan tongues of southern Mexico and was, therefore, well prepared to report on related speech materials in Guatemala. While gathering materials for this book on Jacaltenango, he and Byers took an eight-day pack trip north and then east to other Mayan towns, one of which was Santa Eulalia where La Farge returned in 1932. Fifteen years after his second visit there, he published his study of this village. The last book he wrote as an ethnologist reveals a more mature scientist, if not a more zealous one.

# Opinionated Ethnology:
# A Later View

T HE LOOSELEAF BOOKLET containing the field notes for *Santa Eulalia* was found among the scientific manuscripts in La Farge's studio after his death. The date on the first page of the notebook is February 8, 1932, where there is a statement that Oliver La Farge and Tomas Dozier arrived at the thatch-roofed village of Santa Eulalia "hoping to fill the book to a goodly thickness." The writing is neatly hand printed in ink with chapter headings reading "Agriculture," "Astronomy," "Ceremonies," "Divinities," "Folklore," "Games," "Houses," "Buildings in General," "Material Culture," "Nagualism," "Trade," and "Weaving." All these titles have decorative initial letters in red ink, and the arabic numerals for the chapters are also in red.

Some pages have small blue drawings, and some chapter titles are entirely in red with decorative initials. Sketches of costumes, buildings, and motif designs appear throughout. A miniature dictionary and linguistic phrases along with the texts have been recorded from informants in both Kanhobal and Spanish. There are some stories which also have English translations below each line. The notebook is a model of exactitude plus imagination, and it also indicates that the ability to draw is an asset to an ethnologist. What La Farge wrote in *Santa Eulalia* was applauded as the work of a leading man of science who had also attained eminence as a man of letters.

The printed book does not have the charm of the notebook, because there are no red initials or drawings in red and blue. The chapter headings are more formal, and doubtless the materials in the finished book are more ample, but there is something almost living about a notebook that has been in the hands of a scientist, has been carried in his coat or knapsack, and has made the trip from his study to the field and back again to his study. The sentence

which La Farge writes about himself in the Introduction to the printed book is not found in his field notes. "An amateur scientist and an ardent professional in writing" is the way he describes himself in the Introduction to *Santa Eulalia*. His choice of the word "amateur" is significant. Between 1925 and 1932, he had given as much time to the contemporary Navajos and Mayans as he had given to his novels and short stories. If he had written an introduction to *Santa Eulalia* in 1932 or 1933, would he have called all this labor an effort of an amateur? Postponing a scientific report for fifteen years caused him to feel like an amateur, but the earnestness with which he began his scientific work and the continuity with which he pursued it justify inquiry into what he meant by referring to himself in this way.

He used the term "amateur" again when he received an invitation from the editor of the *Arizona Quarterly* to review papers presented by "professional" anthropologists before meetings of the American Anthropological Association at Tucson in December, 1952.[1] This time he calls himself "a fictioner who happens to be a casual, non-practicing, amateur anthropologist." But La Farge had held appointments as research associate in anthropology at the University of Pennsylvania in 1929-31 and after 1947; at Columbia University, 1930-33; had served as trustee and president of the Museum of Navajo Ceremonial Art in Santa Fe; and had been a member of the Visiting Committee, Department of Anthropology, and the Peabody Museum, Harvard University. The separation he is making distinguishes, therefore, between the scientist who holds a professional salaried post and one who serves on boards of scientific institutions and independently carries on research. To draw a line between an amateur and a professional in these terms is to overlook the dedication of a gifted personality who, whether as a teacher or a researcher under contract, continues to contribute to knowledge of a professional sort. The fact that La Farge was asked to review the work of practicing, therefore professional, anthropologists indicates the recognition accorded to him as an authority in studies relating to the American Indians, especially to those of the Southwestern United States and Central America.

## I  *The Ethnological Standpoint*

During the years devoted to creative writing, La Farge was never

reduced to amateur standing as a scientist. His modest statements to the contrary are not in accord either with the testimonials written about his scientific publications or with the appreciation given his books and articles about the Mayan culture areas. Among his manuscripts are hundreds of pages dealing with such subjects as an alphabet for writing the Navajo language; a plan for the organization of the Hopi tribe in Arizona; the phonetics and vocabularies of Mayan dialects; post-Columbian dates in the Mayan calendar; ethnological data containing measurements of skeletal material from Central America; and voluminous pages on history, ceremony, mythology, and acculturation of Indian groups from the Caribbean jungles to the plateaus of the western United States. There are letters and offprints signed by scientists from the United States, Germany, France, Mexico, and Spain. Summarizing such material is a task too formidable to be undertaken in this chapter, but what can be discussed is the contribution he believed ethnology as a science could make to the advancement of mankind.

In the Introduction to *Santa Eulalia*, La Farge advocated "subjective, even opinionated" ethnological reporting of this Guatemalan village because he thought that ethnology is an inexact science and that it was "inseparable from subjective qualitative observations." He saw no reason why the investigator of intercultural borrowings between diverse peoples should refrain from expressing himself on the success or failure of the process. Therefore, the opinions and the bias of the ethnologist become part of the data found in his report. He condemned colorless objectivity as a faulty technique for workers in this field. He then records his opinions on the success or failure of coffee farms—commercial *fincas*—as they drew natives from the primeval highlands, and his view of machines as they interfered with the "splendid independence" of the natives there.

He evaluated Evangelical missions as spreading confusion in the minds of native Catholics and found the Mayan myths "entertaining" because they mixed Christian lore and doctrine with their fantastic incongruities. As an ethnologist, La Farge liked to see the pagan culture emerge because it was colorful and "native," however barbarous by more civilized standards. At times, though, by implication and irony, he condemned such antique patterns as regressive and as barriers to social welfare; but, whenever possible, he asserted a primary sanction for such ways because of their indige-

ous character. External institutions that brought change were to La Farge subjects of suspicion and distrust.

Some inconsistency, however, may be found here. In the Introduction to *Santa Eulalia*, La Farge in one paragraph briefly surveys the history of quarrels and battles between the villagers and their neighbors. In the next paragraph he refers to their "happy isolation," which presumably permitted them to fight to their hearts' content! To the reader uninitiated in ethnological distinction, some difficulty occurs in associating "happy" with the "general unruliness" he has previously described. A degree of confused subjectivity seems to have guided his scientific opinion.

## II  *The Drama in Ethnology*

La Farge had an instinct for drama, and he makes that clear in both *The Year Bearer's People* and *Santa Eulalia*. The village for which the second book is named was situated at an altitude of 8,300 feet in the great Andean Cordillera across northwestern Guatemala. Magnificent hills and ridges enclosed fertile valleys, and for half the days of the week Santa Eulalia was surrounded by fluffy, white mist that rolled in from the northeast. The church, market, jail, and schools faced into a plaza leveled out of the hillside and surrounded by a hundred houses straggling up the slope. The Indian houses were constructed of poles tied with vines, and the *ladino* or mestizo houses were built of adobe. Thatched roofs were common to both, but shingles or corrugated tin appeared on the roofs of the more prosperous *ladino* houses. At the side or behind the Indian homes were *temascales* or sweat baths, which were small huts partially imbedded in the hillside with a fireplace of rock at one corner and a wide wooden bench at the other. To heat them, a fire was lighted on the stone hearth and allowed to burn down to the coals. When the bather entered, he closed the opening with a thick mat and threw water on the rocks in order to create steam. If he did not desire steam, he could simply bathe in hot water. The *ladinos* had more conventional bathing facilities, but they used the same outdoor kitchens as the Indians, which were sheds separate from the houses where the cooking heat and odors would not reach the interiors. Since the weather was often chilly, family gatherings frequently occured in the kitchen shelters, where there was more warmth than anywhere else.

Upon arriving at Santa Eulalia, La Farge and Dozier moved into one of the better type *ladino* houses. They soon received calls from the other North Americans in Santa Eulalia, one of whom was an Evangelical missionary from a neighboring village; a second visitor was a Catholic priest, also from a neighboring parish. The scientists decided against fraternizing with other North Americans, fearing that such contacts might interfere with establishing close ties with the natives of Santa Eulalia. Gradually they gathered a group of men and boys to take care of the horses and to be their servants. These employees not only helped maintain their household but became loyal and devoted friends, refusing to run away from their employers even during times when they were suspected of exercising an evil influence upon the community.

Every house, Indian or *ladino*, had an outdoor as well as an indoor altar; the outdoor altar was a place to invoke blessings upon the crops, and the indoor altar served for more personal prayers. A little copal and resin placed upon two stones kept incense burning to the outdoor gods, and lighted candles before the cross on the altar inside the house insured the respect due a conventional shrine of worship. La Farge and Dozier were careful to observe all the local customs. Upon meeting the soothsayer in Santa Eulalia, La Farge told him that in the United States he was considered a shaman like the soothsayers in Guatemala. He had come there to learn their rites and practices. La Farge and his group went to light candles and to burn incense in the native manner, participating as fully as was possible in the religious ceremonies of the community.

However, this participation did not remove their party from the risks encountered by the soothsayer when prediction and magic turned out to be wrong. During the last months, the weather in Santa Eulalia had been exceptionally bad. The Fiesta and Easter celebrations were ruined by rain, and the growing season was dry. As a result, the native prayer-makers were blamed; in fact, they were in danger of being placed in jail. The *principal* of the pueblo requested La Farge to make divinations to improve conditions; and, when he refused, the *officiales* decided that he was hostile to the village. To make the situation worse, they accused the Americans of stealing two stone idols from one of the ruins which they had cleared and photographed. Returning to check the spot, the Americans found that the idols really were gone and that a great curse had been placed upon them by the *officiales* of Santa Eulalia. The

ethnologists decided that, in fact, the native prayer-makers had taken the idols in order to discredit the Americans and to shift the blame for bad weather from themselves. Three of the men who were working for the Americans believed the charges and were terrified.

La Farge knew that, if they left the village without having the curse removed, the consequences for his native employees would be very serious. Therefore, he mapped a course of action. First, he told one of his men to go to a soothsayer and tell him to count his seeds (the numerical formula used to check what was favorable in a sequence of twenty days, each of which governed a special type of activity). When the man had performed this ritual, La Farge offered to foretell what his answer would be. In addition, he sent all of his men to make offerings of incense and candles on their private rounds. He himself then prepared to call on the *principal* of the pueblo. After an opening of desultory comments about weather and crops, La Farge abruptly accused the *principal* of lies about his party and of invoking the curse. He reminded the *principal* that a curse improperly laid could react upon those who made it, and he gave the Indian the impression that he, La Farge, had power to reverse the curse and to turn it upon the Indian group and its leaders.

The *principal* of the pueblo was both intimidated and frightened. In the presence of others who had entered the room, he denied that any such spell had been invoked or that he had wished any harm to the Americans and their staff. Wanden La Farge, who had joined her husband in early May, was waiting for him when he returned from the interview with the soothsayer. That night they were awakened by the sound of voices outside the house. They looked through a knothole in the door, saw a group of Indians carrying torches, and heard the Indians talking together. La Farge picked up his shotgun and carried it to the door. He also lit a candle. Then he stood in the candlelight, opening and closing the barrel of the shotgun as noisily as he could. He also raised and lowered the hammer of his revolver a number of times. The commotion inside the house disturbed members of the group outside sufficiently to send them on their way. The La Farges never knew whether they would have proceeded to demonstrate further, but they waited for daybreak with their fears unresolved. On the following day, one of the Indian *officiales* arrived at the house to perform a ritual guaranteeing the Americans a successful trip to the United States.

Thomas Dozier was there when the officer asked Oliver to burn a candle in the cathedral at Guatemala City and accepted money to buy liquor. He explained that his prayers were always better when he had taken something to drink.

This little drama, winding up the visit to Santa Eulalia in 1932, shows how all the details about language, costume, architecture, ritual, and pastime become integrated in thought and behavior. The key to human action and accomplishment lies in motivation; and archaeology, linguistics, folklore, history, geography, and ecology become roads to human appraisal as the ethnologist seeks to diagnose what causes a person to think or act in a particular way. Since La Farge possessed the zeal of a reformer and the imagination of a poet, his practice of ethnology was to "doctor" the emotional as well as the rational needs of people. He became a "medicine man" in as nearly a scientific way as social science made possible.[2]

### III   *What Is Science?*

"What is science?" asks La Farge in the chapter called "The High Plateaux of Asia" from *Raw Material*. "What is the special nature of a scientist as distinguished from a soda-jerker?" Then, in answer, he cites the hours of difficult, dull labor he gave to extracting lists of words, to constructing verb patterns, and to capturing phrases characteristic of native Indian dialects in Mexico and Guatemala. His only textbooks were native speakers, and his schoolrooms were the huts where he met, in one village or another, informants in cold, hot, wet, or dry weather. The hours, days, and weeks jogging on horseback to strange settlements and resting at night on dirt floors were necessary hardships for his scientific labors. Bad food, malaria, dysentery, and threats from illiterate peasants were the risks of research, all in pursuit of a tongue spoken by a few thousand people and of interest to only a dozen or so linguists who would take note of his discoveries and compare them with their own investigations in order to establish the verities of a small corner on the language map of the world.

This pessimistic view of science is the dark side, but the onlooker also shares the brighter view which La Farge enlarges upon. As previously mentioned, he shows how knowledge of a little-known language in Central America could provide a relationship to better known languages in both the New World and the Old and that

they might cast light on the movements of peoples from the high plateaus of Asia through the wastes of the Arctic to the Isthmus of Panama and farther south. A reviewer of *Santa Eulalia* wrote that a highly important by-product of the book was La Farge's discovery of a manuscript at the University Museum in Philadelphia which contained a key to the riddle of Mayan hieroglypic writing.[3]

After a critic writing for the *Bookman* in 1930 asked the question, "Will Oliver La Farge remain an anthropologist?," he then reported a conversation with the curator of a well-known American museum who had just expressed the hope that La Farge's stories would be a "complete flop." He explained this wish by adding: "I don't give a damn about his writings. I don't give a damn for literature. I am interested in science, and he is a first-rate anthropologist. We need him. He's the only man who can talk to the Indians and get anything out of them."[4]

The critic took issue with the scientist by making the point that the scientific background of La Farge made his imaginative work distinctive. Because he was an ethnologist, his novels and stories developed new fields and approaches for serious fiction. Many archaeologists and anthropologists pursued their research and reported on it in an academic way; La Farge not only reported the data but gave it new reality. The probing of human nature in his fiction owed much to the techniques and recording stressed in the laboratory.

## IV   *"I have had to run risks . . ."*

As the techniques of science added a dimension to his writing, so the practice of writing may have contributed a broader vision to his studies in science. Accepting the previously mentioned invitation to review a symposium on the status of southwestern anthropology, La Farge began his review by praising the advances made by "Southwestern studies" since the early days when the reports were limited to archaeology that was chiefly within the "adobe curtain" area, as some writers described it. Today, the broader range includes linguistic geography, anthropometry, folklore motifs, and intercultural exchanges with Plains and Coastal Indians. La Farge urges more attention to history and environmental patterns, whether in pottery design or in creative myths. He urges anthropologists to extend the horizon of their science which had been limited by too

narrow, or specialized fields of research. His view is an over-all one that relates cultural disciplines and includes perimeter geographical areas. La Farge urges his colleagues to supplement their knowledge by drawing more from the humanities—from art, literature, music, and philosophy.

When Oliver was exchanging letters with Margaret Mead about the code of ethics to be adopted by the Society for Applied Anthropology, he wrote:

> I have been involved now for some twenty years in a very active form of applied anthropology. In this I have had to run risks. . . . I believe that my colleagues and myself have been able to do positive good. . . . I feel that the applied anthropologist is an individual engaging in one of the most important, dangerous, and potentially beneficial of all possible forms of tinkering with human life. Unless he has deep conviction, genuine courage, a firm code of ethics, and great clarity of thought, he is unfit for any such undertaking.[5]

La Farge has the qualities he enumerates; and, as a scientist, he chose to express them not only in his scientific works, but also in his novels and short stories. He even chose to put them into his writing of history, when circumstances cast him into a more extensive role as an historian than he ever planned to fill.

CHAPTER **9**

# Ideas Behind the Action: History

L A FARGE DID NOT choose to become an historian in the way of an archivist who writes at a desk in the bookstacks of a library. He consulted records in relationship to what he saw as an anthropologist, searching for the past in terms of the present or, by reversing the viewpoint, tracing the present in terms of the past. He began this type of appraisal when he wrote *As Long as the Grass Shall Grow*, a history combining photography with discussion: the pages of pictures equal exactly the pages of text throughout the book. In 1940 a decade of revolutionary changes had occurred in the program for Indians as conducted by the United States government. American natives had long been viewed as subjects for indoctrination into the Anglo-American way of life. Those who, by choice or necessity, had accepted this situation fared better in the national political and economic scheme than those who resisted conformity. In *As Long as the Grass Shall Grow*, La Farge surveys Indian tribal history and tells a clear story of both mistaken and progressive steps taken by the Indians and by their neighbors.

*The Changing Indian*, as edited by La Farge in 1942, was another book dealing with the social history of Indians, chiefly those living in the United States. Fifteen specialists prepared papers on public health, housing, education, and vocational training for Indians. The difficulties, generally recognized by all the contributors, were those of adjustment between a contemporary and a primitive society, as well as those between a majority and a minority culture of different ethnic groups. The symposium was sponsored by the American Association on Indian Affairs of which La Farge was president. About half of the chapters in this book have photographs relating to a specific topic. *As Long as the Grass Shall Grow* and *The Changing Indian* will be treated together as histories of social changes which La Farge helped to bring about.

# I  *Indians in American Society*

In the Foreword to *The Changing Indian*, La Farge states that for a hundred years the Bureau of Indian Affairs had ignored what science could do to help the native Americans. He does not criticize what may have been good intentions, nor does he disregard the misguided purpose behind such a law as the Allotment Act of 1887, which gave every Indian a specified acreage of land. What he stresses is that, in the two previous decades from 1920 to 1940, science and government had joined to bring new life to both reservation and nonreservation Indians. The first victory, he says, was in public health; then followed improved conservation for grazing and farming lands; finally, changed attitudes toward administration and education had encouraged not only more participation by Indians in managing their economy but also increased appreciation of their own cultural heritage.

John Collier, at this time commissioner of Indian Affairs, who contributed the Introduction to *The Changing Indian*, states that since 1922 new laws had granted full citizenship to Indians in recognition of their World War I services. He adds that other laws had confirmed titles to their lands and established tribal councils to protect water and grazing rights. Finally, he announces that Indian languages, religions, arts, and crafts were now given recognition in order to stabilize them as constructive elements in, or contributions to, the community. Individual writers in *The Changing Indian* point out that the descendants of aboriginal inhabitants in the Western Hemisphere may outnumber their ancestors who were here at the coming of Columbus; that the present population, which is increasing at a higher rate than other groups, will in time require industrialization on the reservations. Vocational education as well as emphasis upon handcrafts may help to support the tribal groups. The concept of a dying way of life has been replaced by that of a revitalized society using the best in the Indian world and adopting what is useful in the non-Indian world.

*As Long as the Grass Shall Grow* concludes with a series of eight photographs, each of which has a caption interpreting the picture. The first, which shows a man attaching a reaper to a tractor, is captioned: "We shall learn all these devices the white man has; we shall handle his tools for ourselves." The next five pictures show Indians who are operating a dragline shovel; working on power lines; threading electrical wires in pipes; arranging surgical tools in a hos-

pital; and sitting at a drafting board. The successive captions are: "We shall master his machinery, his invention, his skills, his medicine, his planning." The last picture portrays a smiling Civilian Conservation Corps worker who joins the other with the words: "And . . . still . . . be Indians."

In 1956, La Farge wrote the most ambitious of his nonfictional works about the aboriginal dwellers in the Western Hemisphere. It was called *A Pictorial History of the American Indian* and begins with the crossing of people from Siberia into Alaska more than twenty thousand years ago, for artifacts have been dated from that time in the southwestern United States. La Farge describes the Stone Age in the New World when the first Americans developed indigenous tools, buildings, rituals, mythology, and social institutions. The book, well illustrated with both colored and black-and-white pages, has such typical chapters as "They Discovered America," "The Old Settlers," "The Great Open Spaces," "Behind the Shining Mountains," "Ghosts and Drugs," and "The Non-Vanishing Americans." A German translation of this book appeared in 1966, and in the same year a Special Edition for Young Readers was issued which contained additional material of interest to school-age children.

## II  *The Army Air Transport Command*

La Farge was awarded Guggenheim Fellowships in 1941 and 1945. The first grant came in the year before he entered military service; the second, in the year before he resigned as chief of the Historical Division of the Army Air Transport Command. Two books were written with the help of these grants: *Raw Material* (1942) and *The Eagle in the Egg* (1949). The conclusion may also be drawn that *War Below Zero* (1944) owed its completion to the support of the first Guggenheim grant. Since much of *Raw Material* had previously appeared in magazines, as had Part I of *War Below Zero*, these two books were less taxing upon La Farge than *The Eagle in the Egg*, which was entirely documented during his five years as advisor in military intelligence. Nevertheless, all three volumes were related to his years in uniform.

*Raw Material*, a largely personal narrative, is a frank commentary upon his psychotic experiences in youth and his professional conflict between creative and scientific interests; but the opening

chapter, "In the Expectation of War," and the final one, "Main Line," refer to his war experience. La Farge states, at the outset, that enlistment changed the whole routine of his life. Instead of ordering his day to suit his purposes as a professional writer, he now hopes for a few moments of spare time to give to his personal projects. Instead of a horseback ride to a place of his choice, he now waits for the schedule of a B-24 airplane, the Liberator, which he terms "that grand, loyal plane with its ugly fuselage and its beautiful, long wings." *Raw Material* closes with a statement that asserts that one of the writer's prime functions is to help restore a world in which free writing can exist. He pays tribute to the military group to which he has been assigned and he considers his assignment one of the many lucky events in his life: "I have fallen in love with a bomber; quite literally, a new world has been opened to me."

H. H. Arnold, commanding general of the Army Air Forces, wrote the Foreword for *War Below Zero*. In it, he called the book "a record of adventure and brave action—of endurance, comradeship, and cooperation to uplift the spirit. . . . It is a story of sterling American qualities which typify our country's airmen." The first part is a reprint of "Greenland Adventure" by Col. Bernt Balchen and Maj. Corey Ford, who relate how an Army Air Force Base on the ice cap of Greenland had been destroyed by German commandos and then recaptured by Americans after a heavy bombing by army planes.

Part II, "The Long Wait," was written by Major La Farge after three men had told him how they survived for five months in a wrecked Flying Fortress. A fourth man, an Army Air Force captain, told of their rescue from one of the most inaccessible places in the Northern Hemisphere, a sheet of ice nine thousand feet thick at the center and only a few hundred feet at the edges. The Flying Fortress had fallen on a plateau which was surrounded by darkness through most of the winter. Vicious winds blasted at the hulk of the B-17, which provided the shelter where the men were snowed in. Deep crevasses crossed the terrain and were often concealed by thin layers of ice and snow. Of the nine members of the crew, one fell into one of these crevasses; another was killed when he returned to help his companions after once having been flown out. A third lost both feet from the gangrene which followed freezing them. The pilot and the radioman also died when the first rescue plane fell. Thus, five men were lost, and seven were saved from this midwinter tragedy, a drama played at first against a background of white snow

with rocky black edges and finally acted in total darkness. The story exemplifies the risks men take to save their fellow men through sacrifice and courage.

Parts III and IV, though not so numbered, are "Postscript" by Lt. Harry L. Smith, and "Life on the Greenland Ice Cap" by Sgt. H. N. Oliphant. The first report is in the form of a diary which the flier kept from July 4 to July 24, 1942. In these three weeks, a squadron of P 38's and B 17's flies over the ice cap to Labrador and then out to the west coast of Greenland. Lieutenant Smith calls the Labrador base a "hellhole with slimy chuck, knotty beds, and an enemy squadron of 109's disguised as mosquitos," adding "a guy who is stationed here insists the mosquitos have so much of his blood in them that they sent him a card on Father's Day." On July 15, six of the planes encountered bad weather and made crash landings in the snow. The twenty-five men, separated into two groups, made themselves as much at home as possible in two of the B-17's which they named *Hotel Dodo* and *Hotel Big Stoop*. Dog sleds were driven to the improvised shelters on July 24th, and the men were then taken to the bay where ships were waiting. The author concludes: "The steak those Navy boys gave us aboard the cutter. That was true love. Spider said, 'Brother, you can say that again.' "

The final story by Sergeant Oliphant tells how he and six others felt about living thirty-five weeks at an army weather and rescue station in Greenland where they were literally imprisoned in the snow. Two of them, however, went to the rescue of the crew of the B 17 described in "The Long Wait" earlier in the book. One of these, Lt. Max H. Demorest, fell through the ice as he guided a propeller-driven sled; the other reached the B-17 on a dog sled. He was Staff Sergeant Tetley, whom Lieutenant Oliphant makes very real as he tells how the sergeant entertained the others with a guitar he made from plywood, glue, and wire. One of the most exciting events during the stay was the birth of four puppies to the station mascot. The man who guessed the right number of births was given a week's vacation from kitchen chores. When the group returned from the ice cap, the colonel asked one of them what he thought of the place. After a moment's hesitation, the man answered: "Well, sir, I'll tell you. It's a nice place to visit, but I wouldn't want to live there." [1]

General Arnold also wrote a Foreword for *The Eagle in the Egg*, calling the book the "unembellished record of a gauntlet flung to the

Impossible," in reference to the overwhelming demands which came from the four corners of the earth for United States military aircraft. [2] Pasted inside the covers of the book is a map of the five continents with lines showing the routes of travel used by the Army Air Transport Command. Across land masses, over vast spaces of water, via islands and stretches of coastline, the Transport Command and the Ferrying Command supplied the Allied armies in days and hours when support by land or by sea would have taken months and weeks. The network of routes enveloped the world. Blind landing systems were evolved, and other technical advances were made to support long-range navigation by air.

In the Foreword, General Arnold said that La Farge's account was "unembellished" because of the absence of light or nonessential details. However, La Farge could not overlook some stories that served to illustrate the rivalry between the army, the navy, and the air force as they tried to specialize and solve all the problems with their own equipment. When a certain regular army colonel stationed on the West Coast was granted a vacation, he got a free ride to the East from the Naval Air Training Service. The colonel ate his breakfast at the Naval Air Station in Oakland, but he was not pleased with the food served him and complained on three counts: there were no doughnuts for his coffee; the liquid tasted like Postum; and he had to drink it from a mug without any handles.

The complaint resulted in an exchange of letters between the colonel, the West Coast commander of the Naval Air Transport Service, an official at the Pentagon, and a major general of the United States Army. The details of this correspondence made clear that the colonel had been served for only twenty cents—fresh fruit, dry cereal with fresh milk, creamed chipped beef on toast, eggs to order, Parker House rolls, and coffee with cream. In answer to the colonel's request for doughnuts, the commander of Naval Transport Command replied that this "product of the culinary art" did not ordinarily form a part of the breakfast for eleven hundred men because of the time and equipment required to prepare it. Moreover, he stated that the beverage served the colonel was a standard brand of navy coffee, of the density preferred by the average navy man. Finally, he regretted that the navy personnel lacked cups with handles; but he opined that, with or without doughnuts, "seldom did two thin dimes buy so much breakfast." He concluded with

120

the remark that a direct ratio might exist between the density of the coffee and that of the man who consumed it.[3]

*The Eagle in the Egg* condenses the records from fifty volumes of documents amassed by workers in the Historical Division of the Air Transport Command. The organization of detail is extraordinary. The index is a guide to staff divisions, officials in charge, airfields, types of planes, the crashes in air traffic and the causes, pilots (both men and women fliers), and the Naval Transport Service in cooperation with the Army Air Transport Command. When La Farge left the service, he was awarded the Legion of Honor with Commendation Ribbon for his work in military intelligence.

### III   *Regional History*

History as pure documentation is found in the last book La Farge prepared, *Santa Fe: The Autobiography of a Southwestern Town* (1959), a collection of news items from the columns of the *New Mexican*. He collaborated with Arthur N. Morgan, a veteran newspaper man, and they arranged selections which began with an item on November 28, 1849, stating that Navajos, Apaches, and Utes were raiding the Territory of New Mexico. The book ended with a report on December 2, 1953, that Zuñi Indians of New Mexico were teaching a troop of Boy Scouts from La Junta, Colorado, to perform Indian dances using authentic steps and costumes. Within this span of years, they found news of such regional events as the voting for delegates to a New Mexican Constitutional Convention on May 5, 1850; the recruiting of soldiers on November 7, 1863, to defend the Territory from raids by both the Confederate soldiers and the Indians; the naming of a Santa Fe street on April 6, 1866, for the late President Lincoln; the proclamation on December 14, 1880, by Governor Lew Wallace of a reward for the capture of desperado Billy the Kid; and the announcement eight days later that the first edition of Wallace's *Ben Hur* had been sold out. *Santa Fe: The Autobiography of a Southwestern Town* is a guide to people and events throughout western as well as southwestern America.

In his approach to the writing of history, La Farge looked for ideas behind social change; and he stressed the part individuals played as progressive or destructive influences. He submerged his personality more in these books than in the novels or short stories. Two books which were essentially marked by his personality appeared after his death: the first, *The Door in the Wall* (1965),

121

is a collection of the last short stories; the second, *The Man with the Calabash Pipe* (1966), is a collection of newspaper essays from the "Bird-Watcher" column. These essays were selected by the poet Winfield Townley Scott, a long-time friend, who was also a Rhode Islander before he moved to Santa Fe. The Calabash-man is a character created as a sounding board for the columnist's own ideas; but, on some of his visits to the columnist's study, the sounding board becomes an adversary. Between them, they manage to present the pro and con of many topical matters of interest to the columnist and his readers.

## CHAPTER 10

# The Crystal in the Bag: Summary

N O one would deny that La Farge was a controversial figure, for he often challenged accepted opinions. When the *Santa Fe New Mexican* invited him to "try his hand" as a newspaper columnist, no limitations were placed on what he chose to write except those against libel and bad taste. The risk of such taste was unnecessary for a man of Oliver's judgment, but the threat of libel was a barrier easy to cross for a man with strong convictions. La Farge never crossed it, but his Sunday "Bird-Watcher" column frequently drew letters to the editor in support of, or in objection to, the opinions he expressed. It is doubtful that any project he ever pursued brought him more pleasure than his newspaper column, even though he often prepared it hastily and without the deliberation that may have been called for. However, the appeal that most columns in newspapers have for their readers lies in the fact that the topics are timely; the issues, controversial; the style, informal; and the opinions, seemingly contemporaneous. La Farge was fifty years old when he undertook this assignment; and whether voicing his thoughts on politics, literature, or art, the judgments are those of maturity. Only those columns that illustrate his breadth and discernment are, however, discussed.

## I  *Chautauqua and Pioneer Mothers*

A good many years before La Farge considered living in Santa Fe—that is, while he was an assistant in ethnology at Tulane—an organization of Texas women proposed to establish a Chautauqua-type settlement for the summer programs near the artist colony in Santa Fe. Several thousand annual visitors planned to make reservations for weeks of cultural refreshment, and the city council heartily favored the project. Opposing the visitors were the permanent artists and writers who appeared before the businessmen and the council to persuade them that casual visitors throughout the sum-

mer could do more for the economy than the planned semiperma-
nent encampment. In a column written to commemorate this event,
La Farge recalled the invasion by the clubwomen and cheered the
victory of the artists. His position seems to have been that organizing culture for club members as a summer pastime might rob it of
any true value.

He also reminded his readers of another controversy in which
he had considered the artist colony a victor. This reference was to
the competition initiated by the Daughters of the American Revolution for a statue depicting a pioneer mother holding a child and
marching over the Santa Fe Trail. The award-winning model was
to be cast in cement, and these copies were to be distributed to
cities and towns along the furrowed trace (now the railroad line
and motor-court route). In each of these communities the Daughters of the American Revolution were to raise money for the trans-
portation and installations of the monuments. The stance of the
figure and the swirl of her dress suggested progress with the wagon
train. In Santa Fe the statue was slated for the central plaza of the
city; but,when leading artists and writers opposed the project, the
figure was sent to Albuquerque, sixty miles to the south, where
today the bonneted mother with windswept skirts, one child in her
arms and another at her side, faces west along the federal highway
through a city park.[1]

La Farge continued to lead the fight to preserve his town as a
retreat and rendezvous for creative spirits; but, during his lifetime
there, the city doubled and trebled in population as commercial
activities increased. He joined the group which refused to surrend-
er the old, artistic districts of Santa Fe to industry or business.
While the town was small, the creative minority had kept the streets
narrow and mainly unpaved and had maintained the dominant
Spanish-Indian style of architecture. This group formed the Old
Santa Fe Association, going so far as to purchase some of the land-
marks and to preserve others. In a column labeled "City Seems
Bent on Suicide," La Farge called the Latin-American charm of
New Mexico's capital city its greatest asset.[2] As in many communities, those who battled for tradition won a few battles and lost as
many. Leadership like that offered by La Farge was notable and
appreciated.

## II  *"Correct" English*

An area of controversy in which Oliver felt especially qualified

was the use of the English vocabulary. In a column written after the publication of *Webster's Third International Dictionary* during the fall of 1961, he criticized the circumlocutions of style of government writers and the "pedagoguese" of educators. His partner in this dialogue is the Man with the Calabash Pipe, whose ideas were as controversial as those of the "Bird-Watcher." After this correspondent leaves, La Farge mulls over the gist of their conversation and turns to a reissue of H. W. Fowler's *Modern English Usage*; he commends Fowler for protecting English speech from the modern heresy that any way of saying a thing is as good as some other. At this point, La Farge seems to lapse into a conservatism which was unscientific, perhaps a throwback to the discipline of Groton days: "We seem to have fallen into a habit of speech that could be called 'approximate English,' or 'near-miss English.' For instance, the words 'disinterest' and 'uninterest' look similar. Their correct meanings are not at all similar, but it is a common practice now to use 'disinterest' to mean 'uninterest.' What word such a user will employ when he wants to say 'disinterest' I know not. Perhaps the concept is too lofty for him to have an occasion to express it."[3]

La Farge must have known as a linguist that there is nothing any more absolutely correct about a word than there is about an ethnological ritual or an aboriginal moral taboo, for language is as evolutionary as any other human practice. Although regional customs and preferences have standardized some sounds and meanings, these have no universal authority over sounds and meanings established elsewhere. The word "disinterest" is composed of a Latin prefix which has such shading of meanings as "in different directions, apart, asunder, away, between, among, though," even plain "not." As the *Oxford English Dictionary* traces the word, "disinterest" entered the language in the seventeenth century as verb, adjective, and noun with meanings as varied as "prejudiced, contrary to interest, devoid of interest, stripped of concern, detached from, without interest," and "unbiased by personal concern." Any speaker or writer may prefer the last meaning and reject all the others, but he cannot find any logical basis for castigating other speakers or writers who choose the meaning "lacking in interest." Etymology, history, and wide usage support both meanings; if La Farge had pursued his investigation more thoroughly, his pronouncement would have been less arbitrary.

In a similar vein, he found fault with the diction of certain an-

thropologists when he reviewed their papers. He rebuked them for careless literary style, pointing out that some used proper names with faulty reference, as in the case of "Hopi are" instead of "Hopis are." He argued that they would not write "Swede are." Yet, as a stylist, he overlooks the collective content in many names which render them singular or plural, depending upon the interpretation of the user. English sportswriters report that a cricket team "have scored" so many runs and a boating crew "are in the lead" by so many yards. American sportswriters, who consider the athletic group to be a unit, select a singular verb: the football team "has a lead" of so many touchdowns. An anthropologist who chooses to write that "the Bengali are" might prefer "Hopi" to "Hopis." In rejecting "Hopi," La Farge disagreed with his old master, Frans Blom, who in *Tribes and Temples* wrote such lines as "the Maya could have gone south" and "the Maya took advantage of," whereas La Farge in *The Year Bearer's People* always wrote "the Mayas of Yucatan" and "among the Mayas." The subtleties of language yield to stylistic preference but rarely to dogma.

Oliver's concern for the proprieties of words bespoke his true love for his native tongue. When he lamented the slow, current decay of English, it is only because he overlooks what happened to English in Geoffrey Chaucer's day or even in Shakespeare's. He believed that the adverb was disappearing because Americans have accepted "go slow" for "go slowly," yet in early English many adverbs, perhaps a majority, ended in vowel sounds which in time ceased to be pronounced. As a result, "go slow" is an older expression than "go slowly." There are no older English adverbs than those that remain in groups like "drive fast, hit hard, jump high, throw far, aim low, run quick, live long" and others of their kind. Despite his pessimism, La Farge spoke of English as "a writer's dream language" and called American English "wonderful, a delight to speak and to write in its enormous variety, range, and flexibility."[4]

## III  *Zip Codes*

To classify Oliver's objections to zip codes is a problem. Because he was a champion of human rights, he was opposed to machines when they invaded areas reserved for personal command. As human controls waned, La Farge's temper waxed. The reader can almost feel the severity with which he wrote: "These numbers make no sense in themselves. Any sorter, any human sorter, that is, can make

more sense out of 'Idaho' at the bottom of a letter than out of a senseless conglomeration of digits. The point of conditioning us to these digits, of getting us to help dig our own prison by circulating these numbers, can only be in future automation." He complains that Americans are already afflicted with too many digits: street numbers, telephone numbers, other people's numbers, army serial numbers, veterans' files, and social-security numbers. Then he concludes: "That, ladies and gentlemen, is quite sufficient."[5]

Doubtless, as time passed, the Zoning Improvement Plan of sorting mail would have won his support. Hostility to codes which pinpointed and classified humanity simply illustrated his posture in the losing battle against a world in which an ethnologist was not competitive. How does a social scientist fight a computer? Applied anthropology will surely decide to make use of automation rather than to oppose it.

## IV  *Jung and the Cave Man*

On scientific topics La Farge was justifiably disputatious. Late in the third year of his "Bird-Watching," he wrote a column taking issue with his colleague who had applied the psychology of Carl Jung to the habits of primitive man. Since many traces of early habitation by the human race in Europe were found in caves, theorists reasoned that in the glacial period extreme cold had driven men and their families under ground. From these facts developed the myth of Cave Man. The Jungians added as a hypothesis that people chose to live in caves because they recalled the security of the wombs where they were developed; therefore, they sought to return to the state of prebirth. La Farge pointed out that whatever security there may have been in caves was offset by the lack of sanitation and dampness. The remains of Homo sapiens which have been found not only in Europe, but in Asia and Africa as well, have as often as not been outside caves as in them. The Jungian hypothesis about the womb quest of early man must be filed away with the ponderings of the ancient Greek philosophers, "speculating brilliantly with logic and imagination, free of the mean and constricting bondage of fact."[6]

## V  *Holly and Clam Chowder*

The newspaper columnist began in England, during the days of Addison and his *Spectator* when an essayist could choose to discuss

whatever came into his mind. In this easygoing free-wheeling vein, Oliver was at his very best. His temper was unroiled and his tempo rollicksome. As an ex-Rhode Islander, he wanted to import holly from his native state, believing that it would flourish in Santa Fe. "That's a good tree," he writes of holly: "Its green leaves shine all winter and the snow on them makes fascinating patterns. In the spring the blossoms perfume the air all around, and they are great providers for bees. A bird that nests high in holly is relatively safe from cats." But there was more to the atmosphere of New Mexico to encourage holly than just the clear air and bright sunshine: holly flourishes on romance. The female plant must have a mate. So the "Bird-Watcher" concludes: "To do well, hollies must have a satisfactory love life, and of course that is the kind of thing that creates difficulties in New England. Out here, hollies with a Latin touch, uninhibited hollies so to speak, might thrive exceptionally well."

Another Rhode Island transplant found a place in his column several months later. Perhaps he encountered other New Englanders who had strayed from their old homesites, for he writes of discussing with one of them how clam chowder should be made. As a native of the "chowder belt," La Farge says that he had learned the art of preparing chowder while under sail on salt water and that there was no other place as authentic to learn it. The first thing about preparing chowder is to know what to leave out. Tomatoes should never be put in the soup! The bystander is amazed at the vehemence expressed on this point. Tomatoes in chowder are a "vile, base, unwarranted libel" on the true dish. He accuses Fannie Farmer, author of the well-known cookbook, of being a Massachusetts "fifth columnist" in permitting tomatoes to appear in what she calls the "Rhode Island recipe." After his diatribe against tomatoes, "something that doesn't know whether it's a fruit, vegetable, or a berry," he never bothers to recite what to put into the chowder brew. Presumably, the reader will have to visit Newport or Saunderstown or sail a boat on salt water to discover how clam chowder should be made and how it should taste.[7]

## VI  *"Liberal" and "Conservative"*

Other informal essays of charm and sentiment appear in his column. One of them describes the comfortable disarray of a house in which an active child has been at work or play; another argues that

the United States learned a lesson in tolerance when John Fitzgerald Kennedy was elected president; a third reminisces about the seasonal holidays, Thanksgiving, Christmas, and New Year's Day; finally, one of the most worthwhile discusses the types of mind called "liberal" and "conservative."

The conservative individual, according to La Farge, is the man who wishes to save existing values, to retain the basic and familiar way of doing things, believing them essential to the preservation of democracy since they have contributed to stability, law, and order. This conservative is not an extremist or a reactionary who objects to change if an old pattern has outlived its day. In contrast, a liberal has the imagination to see inequities in an established social system and to construct a new pattern for correcting them when they are revealed. He is not a radical, calling for total destruction of the status quo in order to reform what has been a failure. A liberal founds his political faith upon the same basic principles of American democracy that a conservative does, but he stresses greater equality of privilege among the members of society and full participation of the government in bringing about economic as well as political integration. Each political type should be within debating distance of the other.

Therefore, in the opinion of the "Bird-Watcher," there can be in the United States such a political being as a liberal conservative and a conservative liberal.[8] Indeed La Farge found himself in both camps. Liberal in some respects and conservative in others, he crossed the battle lines as he saw fit. Instinctively a traditionalist, he tried to blaze new trails for the Indian programs of the government. Conformist by training, he fought standardization and mechanization when either process curbed creative action and freedom of expression. His mind and his pen were never at rest so long as there was a cause each could serve and he was well enough to put them to work. A "Bird-Watcher" is ever faithful to his watching, and he has his favorites among the birds.

## VII  *The Achievement of Oliver La Farge*

Oliver La Farge appeared upon the literary scene in the late 1920's when novels were being read in greater numbers than ever before. He published his first novel in what has been called the "age of gold" for best-selling fiction. *Laughing Boy* arrived in the same year with *The Magnificent Obsession* by Lloyd C. Douglas,

*Dodsworth* by Sinclair Lewis, and *All Quiet on the Western Front* by Erich Maria Remarque. The story about the Navajos may not have equaled the immediate sales of its popular rivals, but it was competitive, and in the long stretch may have surpassed one or all of them. Artistically, it still holds its own with each. *Sparks Fly Upward* fought in 1931 for a share of the market with Pearl Buck's *The Good Earth*, Willa Cather's *Shadows on the Rock*, and Ellery Queen's *The Dutch Shoe Mystery*. *Long Pennant* (1933) had as rivals Hervey Allen's *Anthony Adverse*, James Hilton's *Lost Horizon*, and Caroline Miller's *Lamb in His Bosom*. *The Enemy Gods* (1937) claimed readers' dollars at a time when Archibald Cronin's *The Citadel*, J. P. Marquand's *The Late George Apley*, and John Steinbeck's *Of Mice and Men* were also bidding. The public was drawn more strongly to Franz Werfel's *The Song of Bernadette* and to another Lloyd C. Douglas success, *The Robe*, than it was to La Farge's *The Copper Pot* (1942).

If competition in these years with such popular rivals was a problem for a scientist turned novelist, it was also a challenge, for world attention had been focused upon American literature. The awarding of three Nobel Prizes to Americans for literature in the 1930's proclaimed the stature of American writing: Sinclair Lewis, 1930; Eugene O'Neill, 1936; and Pearl Buck, 1938. The perspective of a quarter of a century may shade the comparative value in all three authors and their individual works, but no time interval can ignore the literary trend or emphasis to which they contributed.

The decade between 1920 and 1930 had been in the realistic mold. Sinclair Lewis in his best sellers, *Main Street, Babbitt,* and *Elmer Gantry*, caricatured taste, business ethics, and religion in rural America. John Dos Passos transferred such satire to the cities with the camera shots and newsreel treatment he developed in *Manhattan Transfer* and in *42nd Parallel*. James T. Farrell had just begun to write his early short stories with their corrosive exploration of moral decadence in the Chicago South Side background of his young hero Studs Lonigan. The stream-of-consciousness technique became a symbol of disintegration for a world which never would have been recognized as American by writers who had finished all or most of their work before this time, such as James Lane Allen, Emerson Hough, Jack London, Owen Wister, Edith Wharton, Booth Tarkington, and Stewart Edward White. These early novelists saw more light than shadow in the life around them and still

found the individuals in their books more responsible for their faults than the society in which they lived. Theodore Dreiser maintained that he had no philosophy, but the vast pity of *An American Tragedy*, which appeared in 1925, did not purge the social conscience for the aimlessness of purpose in the life of Clyde Griffiths, the underprivileged boy who is the victim of class discrimination and economic inequality in his environment.

Earnest Hemingway and William Faulkner, the titans of the decade from 1930 to 1940, were little, if any, more optimistic about the human race than the novelists of the previous ten years; but there was new depth of psychological analysis in characterization and increased skill in portraying the tensions the characters faced. Realism in the world as they pictured it was mixed with poetic quality. Society was searching for a new identity and seeking release from the materialism that had engulfed it. Perhaps "poetic realism" is the phrase to describe the mood induced by these creative artists. Thornton Wilder and Thomas Wolfe contributed to it, as did Edna Ferber, who infused the colorful scenes of historical backgrounds with the challenge of venturesome incidents.

Poetic realism, colorful scenes, and historical backgrounds were important in the imagination of Oliver La Farge. His Introductory Note to *Laughing Boy* was signed "New Orleans, 1929," but he had spent the better part of five previous summers in Arizona and New Mexico, where he had become familiar with the folklore and ethnology recorded by such writers as Washington Matthews, Frank Cushing, Adolph F. Bandelier, Charles Fletcher Lummis, Edgar Lee Hewett, and Elsie Clews Parsons. These scientists with literary skills had laid the foundations for a school of regional writing; they were both measurers and imaginers, scholars and creators. Their reports were readable as well as statistical, and nearly all of them had written for a general as well as a specialized audience. Bandelier dramatized the romance and rivalries in prehistoric Indian days of two American continents with his novels *The Delight Makers* and *The Gilded Man*. *The Delight Makers* has its scenes among the cliff dwellings at El Rito de Los Frijoles canyon, now a National Monument twenty miles west of Santa Fe. Where could a young scientist like La Farge with creative imagination have found a more hospitable environment?

The two La Farge novels which have uniqueness are *Laughing Boy* and *The Enemy Gods*, with their semiarid world of valleys,

131

ancient ruins, and primitive peoples encircled by the railroads, high-
ways, and cities of the twentieth century. The author was never entirely satisfied with his first novel; for, when the book was reissued in
paperback thirty-three years after the first printing, he called it the
work of a young man who was rather "ferocious" and "romantic"
about these Indians and what modern civilization had done to their
way of life. As a social scientist, he had lived on their reservation
and had learned of their friendly characteristics and rich ceremonial
faith in both sickness and health. Because the tribe was then disappearing, he had felt that his book might picture its culture and help
to preserve the mystical faith in a nonmaterial world where peace
triumphed over strife, beauty over ugliness. As time passed, however, the Navajos did not disappear. Instead, they grew into a
powerful community more than twice the previous size; these
Indians became involved in politics, money, and all the tools of
civilization. As a result, La Farge calls them an unhappy people,
unfriendly toward others, with only a trace of the beauty and sense
of fun, the wholeness he described in *Laughing Boy*. This last view
of the Navajos is touched with disillusion, but it is doubtful that the
critics of the novel in 1929 would retract the words they wrote in
its favor or that readers now would disparage what they said. Almost
without exception, they stressed the poetic style of the author, his
love of nature, and the mysterious beauty of the civilization to
which he transported the reader.[9]

Harlan Hatcher writes that La Farge joined with Thornton
Wilder, Elizabeth Madox Roberts, Willa Cather, and others in
establishing a vein of poetic perception in narrative prose, a medium
which could deal effectively with the rich, historic traditions of
the nation.[10] The Kentucky of Miss Roberts, the Nebraska of Miss
Cather, and the South of Margaret Mitchell demanded an imaginative style, one sensitive to themes and settings such as those that
Hemingway, Fitzgerald, and the other expatriate literati were
searching to find in France, Italy, and Spain. The Americans who
sought backgrounds and plots among distinctive racial groups at
home were called "provincial," and a tendency developed to slight
their novels as "regional." By contrast, similar works located in
villages or urban quarters of England, France, or Italy were ac-
claimed as "international" and "cosmopolitan." But all could be
tagged as equally regional if their writings are distinctive of a place,
stamped by a vocabulary peculiar to a group, and motivated by cir-

cumstances determined by that locality and its customs.

All novelists, except those who deal in fantasy, become ethnologists. Their ethnological worlds may be fictitious; but, if they deal with customs and actions of people, the books are ethnology of a sort. La Farge created such worlds in nineteenth- and twentieth-century settings for New England seafarers (*Long Pennant*), a southwestern Indian tribe (*Laughing Boy, The Enemy Gods*), pure bloods and *ladinos* in Central America (*Sparks Fly Upward*), and Louisiana sophisticates (*The Copper Pot*). In each of these studies, the characters came from an environment with significant meaning; and this significance is deepened, enlarged, or redirected by the experiences reported in the stories. None of the lives is aimless; each acquires purpose—to shape a destiny. Even when the outcome is tragic, the loss finds compensation through the intention of the loser; or it brings fulfillment to those with whom the characters have been associated.

The twenty-four titles listed in the bibliography of books by Oliver La Farge can be divided equally into fiction and nonfiction. The same thread of purposefulness runs through them all. No one reader is likely to read every book he wrote, but a glance at the titles alone shows the quality of affirmation in the contents of the books. Such words as "Temples, People, Art, Sparks, Pennant, Young Men, Gods, Alphabet, Grow, Changing, War, Eagle, Mountains, Desert, American" are terms of challenge or accomplishment. They do not suggest defeat or despair, nor doubt and gloom.

## VIII  *The Crystal in the Bag*

Midway in his career, when La Farge tried to record the goals of his writing, he began by stating that "You spend your life in pursuit of something you will never catch . . . the good, the beautiful, and the true. They are all one." Then he assumed that a painter would choose "beauty" for the perfect union of all three and that a writer would select "truth" as the ultimate expression of both beauty and goodness. As a man who was sometimes a poet, sometimes a scientist, and occasionally a painter, he concluded: "I suppose everyone must visualize his objective in his own way. The crystal comparison is the one I think of most, the completely clear, flashing crystal which is also, in different terms and conditions, the goal of science and of religion. The crystal hidden in a medicine bag. Inadequate, but then no visualization or metaphor will serve. You

simply know that it exists and that you are shooting at the North Star with a popgun."[11]

Just before La Farge became ill in the spring of 1963, he had visited Taos to consult with the leaders of the pueblo who for the last fourteen years had been carrying on litigation before the Indian Claims Commission and presenting data to establish title to forest lands northeast of the pueblo. Here the Taos Indians had held sacred rituals before the coming of the Spanish. As they said in their appeal to Congress, "We have no buildings there, no steeples. There is nothing the human hand has made. The lake is our church. The mountain is our tabernacle. The evergreen trees are our living saints. They are with us perpetually."[12] In September, 1965, the Indians heard that the Claims Commission had ruled in their favor and that they would receive a considerable sum of money to compensate them for the use of their land. In March of the following year, a bill was introduced in Congress which would give the pueblo title to a sacred area surrounding the religious assembly sites. The cause for which La Farge labored and wrote until within a few weeks before his death had won a significant battle. The battle was larger than the specific case of Taos, for it showed that the United States, as a nation, respected the rights of minority groups. There would be general recognition for the songs and dances of these Indians, for their poetry, folklore, and religious freedom. The American scene would not lose the beauty and color symbolized by the crystal in the medicine bag.

# Notes and References

## Chapter One

1. Factual material for this chapter was gathered from such references as *Historical and Statistical Gazeteer of New York State* (Syracuse, 1860), pp. 351-54, 360; *Dictionary of American Biography* (New York, 1933), pp. 530-35; *Who Was Who in America*, Vol. I (Chicago, 1943); *New York, A Guide to the Empire State* (New York, 1940); *Rhode Island, A Guide to the Smallest State* (Boston, 1937). The legend of Frederic de la Farge and the rowboat is told by his great-great-granddaughter Povy La Farge Bigbee. Letter, May 2, 1966. The facts may be that he escaped in a rowboat and was picked up by an English frigate.

2. John La Farge and his family are vividly portrayed in the first three chapters of *The Manner Is Ordinary* (New York, 1954), written by his son, John La Farge, S. J., who was an uncle of Oliver La Farge, II. Equally personal slants are found in "Schoolboy Letters between John La Farge and His Father," *Historical Records and Studies*, United States Catholic Historical Society, March, 1928; and *John La Farge* by Royal Cortissoz (1911). A recent appraisal of the work of John La Farge appeared in "Meticulous Mandarin," *Time*, LXXXVII (June 3, 1966), 64.

3. John La Farge, S. J. *The Manner Is Ordinary*, p. 17.

4. *Ibid.*, pp. 389-90; also Grace M. Mayer, *Once Upon a City* (New York, 1958), pp. 456-58. The cathedral is discussed in *Time*, LXXXVIII (December 2, 1966), 75, which reports that a dome of modern styling is now planned instead of the gigantic spire and that the church is exceeded in size only by Saint Peter's Basilica in Rome.

5. This quotation and the two which follow it are taken from a letter by Margaret La Farge Osborn, written to the author on April 6, 1966.

6. *Raw Material* (Boston, 1945), p. 73. This book was published when Oliver La Farge was forty-four years of age. One-third of his life still lay ahead; the book, therefore, could scarcely be called an autobiography. It is neither complete nor sufficiently detailed to serve as a life story, but it does give clues to motivation during the writer's boyhood and early maturity. A good many of his life experiences are richly amplified.

7. *Ibid.*, p. 13.

8. Letter to the author, June 9, 1966, from Walter L. Goodwin, Jr., a member of the Groton class of 1920.

9. Henry Fairfield Osborn, *Men of the Old Stone Age* (New York, 1934), pp. 19, 188. Professor Osborn mentions the Ice Age in North America. Artifacts revealing characteristics of early man have been discovered in the Western Hemisphere, although human remains are still to be found. See Frank Hibben, *The Lost Americans* (New York, 1946, 1947), Chapters 10, 12.

10. "The Eight-Oared Shell," *Harper's Monthly*, CLXXXII (July, 1942), 174-79; also in *Raw Material*, pp. 60-71.

11. Excerpt from typed essay by Douglas B. Byers, "Oliver La Farge," p. 4.

12. Arthur Stanwood Pier, *The Story of Harvard* (Boston, 1903), p. 211.

13. *Raw Material*, pp. 20-21.

14. "Captain Tom and Mother Carey's Chickens," *Harvard Advocate,* CIX (October 1, 1922), 9-13.

15. *Ibid.*, CIX (February 1, 1923), 147-48.

16. *Ibid.*, CIX (March 1, 1923), 212-15.

17. *Ibid.*, CIX (March 1, 1923), 205; CX (October 1, 1923), 9-10.

18. "Navajo Folk Tales," *Journal of American Folklore*, XXXVI (1923), 368-75.

19. "Baccalaureate Hymn," with permission of F. A. O. Schwartz, Jr., who holds the copyright for the Twenty-fifth Anniversary Report.

20. Douglas S. Byers, *op. cit.*, p. 3.

## Chapter Two

1. *The Copper Pot* (Boston, 1942), p. 233. The rest of the quotation is: "But you learn a lot by doing it; it had made him dig into his own reasons. At school the Head was always saying, '*Dociendo discimur,*' and it was true."

2. *Raw Material*, p. 168.

3. *Tribes and Temples* (New Orleans, 1926), pp. 248, 445, 501. *Tata* is Yocotan, a dialect of Chontol which is of Mayan stock. Among the Pueblo Indians of the United States, there is a word *taytay,* meaning "grandfather." See Elizabeth Willis De Huff, *Taytay's Tales* (New York, 1922), p. vii. *Tata* is defined as American colloquial Spanish for "daddy" in Appleton's *New Spanish Dictionary* (1931) and a familiar term for "little brother" in Mafer's *Diccionario de la Lengua Castellana con Mexicanismos* (1944).

4. Statement on cover jacket, *The Copper Pot* (1942).

5. "Oliver La Farge 2nd Likes Life in Rhode Island," *Providence Bulletin*, November 12, 1932.

6. "Oliver La Farge, 61, Well-Known Writer, Dies in City Hospital," *Albuquerque Journal*, August 3, 1963.

# Notes and References

## Chapter Three

1. Interview, Wanden Kane, July 23, 1966, at Fountain, Colorado. Wanden La Farge was the author of "No Turtles Need Apply," *Saturday Evening Post*, CCXI (July 9, 1938), 18-19.

2. Interview, Franc J. Newcomb, March 10, 1966, at Albuquerque, New Mexico. Mrs. Newcomb was the author of *Navajo Omens and Taboos* (Santa Fe, 1940), *Hosteen Klah* (Norman, 1964), and *Navajo Neighbors* (Norman, 1960).

3. Foreward to Sentry paperback edition of *Laughing Boy* (Boston, 1962).

4. *New Orleans Times-Picayne*, January 24, 1932; a picture shows La Farge directing the heroine in attitudes and gestures appropriate to Navajo Indians.

5. *Detroit Free Press*, March 9, 1932; *Providence Journal*, November 10, 1932.

6. Interview, Wanden Kane, previously cited; also Philip Friedman, "Oliver La Farge, The Scientist as Literary Artist," p. 19. Unpublished M.A. thesis, 1959.

7. *Gallup Independent*, January 20, 1933.

8. "Indians to be Present at Dinner Here Tonight," *New York Sun*, April 17, 1934.

9. Interview, Consuelo La Farge, September 14, 1966: the name of the journalist was Brian Boru Dunne, who interviewed, over a period of forty years, almost every visitor of interest to Santa Fe. He usually encountered them in the lobby of this hotel.

## Chapter Four

1. "He claimed an inheritance of the North American Indian in his family descent and was proud of it as well as quite definite to the point of making some of the rest of us feel there was something wrong because we didn't have it or hadn't thought of it ourselves in advance. He was quite dark and this added to the veracity of the claim. He also walked in a rather peculiar pidgeon-toed way which we assumed all Indians used because they were not accustomed to shoes." Letter, Walter L. Goodwin, Jr., previously cited. "There is a family legend that we have some Indian blood, though no one has ever been able to pin it down." Letter, Margaret La F. Osborn, previously cited. "My Great-Great-Great-Grandfather's Battle," *New Yorker*, XXV (August 13, 1949), 72, may shed light on the subject.

2. *The Man with the Calabash Pipe* (Boston, 1966), pp. 8-10.

3. Letter to La Farge dated July 31 and containing a reference "as of August, 1940"; the writing paper has *The New Republic* letterhead.

4. "No More Bohemia," *Harper's Bazaar*, No. 2670 (April, 1935), p. 188; also *All The Young Men* (Boston and New York, 1935), p. 272. *The*

*Copper Pot*, pp. 236-95, reprints "No More Bohemia" almost word for word, except that the hero in the novelette comes from Vermont instead of Rhode Island and tells the story in the first person. There are other slight changes in the plot.

5.  Henry H. Richards, retired Groton master, writes: "In a 1947 report La Farge says that he won a school letter in rowing. He must have been a substitute on the school crew and have rowed in some race that 'counted.'"

6.  "Bird-Watcher" column, *Santa Fe New Mexican*, January 8, 1950.

7.  "Fiesta in Tucson," reprinted in *News Week* from report in *Tucson Daily Citizen*, April 9, 1951; also the *Arizona Daily Star*, April 8, 9, 1951.

8.  Letters, Margaret Mead to La Farge, December 12, 1951; La Farge to Miss Mead, January 15, 1952.

9.  "Bird-Watcher" column, December 28, 1952; also *The Man with the Calabash Pipe*, pp. 236-38.

10.  Interview, Karl Laarson, Santa Fe, June 6, 1966. Laarson was the illustrator of *The Mother Ditch* (Boston, 1954).

11.  Articles from Santa Fe and Washington, D.C., as reprinted in the *Albuquerque Journal* for August 12 and August 15, 1962.

12.  "Bird-Watcher" column, *Santa Fe New Mexican*, July 30, 1961; material also in *Albuquerque Journal*, May 19, 1966, p. C-8; and in *Albuquerque Tribune* of the same date on p. B-12.

13.  Interviews, Consuelo La Farge, June 8, 1965; Povy La Farge Bigbee, July 15, 1966; and Dr. R. E. McQuigg, Lovelace Clinic, Albuquerque, November 3, 1966. The death certificate, signed on August 2, 1963, specifies thrombosis of the right pulmonary artery. The intern, Dr. Edward B. Solomon, who attended La Farge at Bataan Hospital, pays tribute to his "down-to-earth, casual, friendly" behavior as a patient. He also states that his smoking aggravated the emphysema. Letter, October 10, 1966, Palo Alto-Stanford Hospital Center, California.

14.  *Raw Material*, p. 101.

15.  "Final Service for La Farge," *Albuquerque Tribune*, August 5, 1963.

## Chapter Five

1.  *An Ethnological Dictionary of the Navajo Language*, p. 450. Saint Michaels, Arizona: The Franciscan Fathers, 1910.

2.  *Raw Material*, p. 201.

3.  *Laughing Boy*, p. 165.

4.  *As Long as the Grass Shall Grow* (New York, 1940), pp. 124-25.

5.  *Raw Material*, p. 211.

6.  *Laughing Boy*, Sentry Edition (1962), p. vii.

7.  *Raw Material*, p. 176.

8.  *Sparks Fly Upward* (Boston, 1931), p. 286.

9. *Ibid.*, p. 47.

10. *Ibid.*, p. 65.

11. "Chog's Cove is a real place, but an invented name. . . . I don't know if it was my brother Christopher, or Oliver that first used it, but I think it was Christopher in a long verse novel he wrote. The place meant a great deal to all of us. We had our own dock and float, and a fine boat." Letter, Margaret La F. Osborn, September 25, 1966. The name appeared in Oliver's *Long Pennant*, which was published before either of Christopher's novels in verse.

12. By the test of monosyllables, *Long Pennant* ranks below all the other La Farge novels, with a percentage of single to multisyllable words of 68.4.

13. *Raw Material*, p. 208.

14. *No More Bohemia*, p. 272. This novel has a 72.5 percentage of monosyllabic words, which places it third (by this standard) in the listing of La Farge novels.

15. Frances Gillmor, chairman of the Folklore Committee, University of Arizona, supplied the material for this statement. She also sent xeroxed pages from the study by Harry Tegnaeus, *Blood-Brothers* (Stockholm, 1952; New York, Philosophical Library, 1953). On page 41 of this study, there is a statement by Elliott Arnold that his account of the pact between Cochise and Jeffords, as presented in his novel *Blood Brother* (New York, 1947), was confirmed by an Apache in Tucson who said he had such a rite performed at his own marriage.

## Chapter Six

1. "Our Empire Authors," by Hugh McGovern, *Santa Fe New Mexican;* found in La Farge Clipping Book, Dated ca. January, 1952.

2. "North Is Black," *Dial*, LXXXII (January, 1927), 8-19; "Women at Yellow Wells," *Saturday Evening Post* CCVII (November 24, 1934), 8-9; both stories are reprinted in *All the Young Men* (1935).

3. All five of the published stories appeared in issues of the *New Yorker* for 1938, Volume XIII, Pts. 1 and 2. The two summarized here are "By the Boys Themselves," May 14, and "The Touch of Greatness," June 4. Three others were "Discovery," February 12; "First Day," March 5; and "Grounds of Offense," March 26. The four unpublished titles are "According to the Rules," "Boundaries of Honor," "The Fein Game," and "Reminder," the first and third of which are dated September, 1940.

4. "Old Century's River," *Atlantic Monthly*, CLXXXVI (September, 1950), 19-25; also in *A Pause in the Desert* (Boston, 1957).

5. "La Spécialte de M. Duclos," *New Yorker*, XXVI (April, 1950), 26-28; also in *A Pause in the Desert*.

6. "Haunted Ground," *Ladies Home Journal*, XLVII (August, 1930),

9; also in *All the Young Men.*

7. "Independent Research," *Esquire,* VIII (August, 1937); also in *The Door in the Wall* (Boston, 1965).

8. "The Resting Place," *New Yorker,* XXX (October 16, 1954), 26-32; also in *A Pause in the Desert.*

## Chapter Seven

1. "Adaptations of Christianity Among the Jacalteca Indians of Guatemala," *Thought,* II (1927), 476-95; "The Ceremonial Year at Jacaltenango," *Proceedings,* Twenty-third International Congress of Americanists (1928), pp. 656-80; "Post Columbian Dates and the Maya Correlation Problem," *Maya Research* (1934), 109-24; "Mayan Ethnology: The Sequence of Cultures," in *The Maya and Their Neighbors* (New York, 1940), pp. 289-94.

2. *Tribes and Temples,* p. 196.

3. *Raw Material,* pp. 89-90.

4. *The Year Bearer's People* (New Orleans, 1931), p. 188.

5. *Ibid.,* p. 186.

6. *Ibid.,* 134.

## Chapter Eight

1. The papers were printed in the "Southwest Issue" of the *American Anthropologist,* LVI (August, 1954), as edited by Emil Haury.

2. *Santa Eulalia* (Chicago, 1947), pp. 185-94.

3. "Keeping Up With Man." Review of *Santa Eulalia: The Religion of a Cuchumatan Indian Town.* Laboratory of Anthropology, Santa Fe, 1949. J. Eric S. Thompson, in *Maya History and Religion* (Norman, 1970), p. xxv, calls La Farge one of the "giants of this century" in Maya research.

4. John Bird, *Bookman,* LXXII (September-February, 1930-31), 11.

5. Letter of La Farge to Margaret Mead, January 15, 1952.

## Chapter Nine

1. *War Below Zero, The Battle for Greenland* (Boston, 1944), pp. 108, 118, 127.

2. *The Eagle in the Egg* (Boston, 1949), p. vi.

3. *Ibid.,* pp. 273-77.

## Chapter Ten

1. *The Man with the Calabash Pipe,* pp. 24-26.

2. *Ibid.,* pp. 40-46; also "Bird-Watcher" column, *Santa Fe New Mexican,* March 7, 1956.

3. *Ibid.*, p. 117.

4. *Ibid.*, p. 118; also "Bird-Watcher" column, January 24, 1954; October 14, 1962.

5. "Bird-Watcher" column, June 30, 1963.

6. *Ibid.*, August 3, 1952; also in *The Man with the Calabash Pipe*, pp. 200-202.

7. *Ibid.*, June 1 and September 21, 1952; also *The Man with the Calabash Pipe*, pp. 173-75, 179-81.

8. *Ibid.*, November 12, 1961; also *The Man with the Calabash Pipe*, pp. 207-9.

9. Clinton Simpson, *Bookman*, LCC (January, 1930), 561; Margaret Wallace, *New York Times*, November 24, 1929, p. 7; I. W. Lawrence, *Boston Transcript,* November 9, 1929, p. 3; *New Republic*, LXI (December 25, 1929), 151.

10. Harlan Hatcher, *Creating the Modern American Novel* (New York, 1935), p. 251.

11. *Raw Material*, p. 210. In Navajo ceremonies, a crystal is considered the symbol of truth. The patient places crystals in several hollow reeds while the medicine man chants prayers of healing. *Navajo Creation Myth*, by Hasteen Klah, as recorded by Mary C. Wheelright (Santa Fe, 1942), p. 23.

12. *Santa Fe New Mexican,* April 24, 1966, pp. B 1-3. The claim of the Taos Indians to Blue Lake and 48,000 acres of forest land was confirmed in a bill signed by President Nixon on December 15, 1970. Title for the Pueblo is held in trust by the secretary of the interior.

# Selected Bibliography

## PRIMARY SOURCES

### 1. Fiction

*All the Young Men.* Boston: Houghton Mifflin, 1935. Contains twelve stories, eleven of which had been published previously: "Hard Winter," "All the Young Men," "Haunted Ground," "A Family Matter," "North Is Black," "Higher Education," "The Goddess Was Mortal," "Dangerous Man," "Love Charm," "Woman at Yellow Wells," "Camping on My Trail," and "No More Bohemia."

*Behind the Mountains.* Boston: Houghton Mifflin, 1956. Somewhat fictionalized chapters of life in a Spanish-American village, all but three of them previously published.

*Cochise of Arizona.* New York: Aladdin Press, 1953. Short novel; semi-historical in plot and development.

*Copper Pot, The.* Boston: Houghton Mifflin, 1942.

*Door in the Wall, The.* Boston: Houghton Mifflin, 1965. Twelve stories about anthropologists, most of whom teach at an imaginary Talvert University. Seven of these stories published previously.

*Enemy Gods, The.* Boston: Houghton Mifflin, 1937.

*Laughing Boy.* Boston: Houghton Mifflin, 1929.

*Long Pennant.* Boston: Houghton Mifflin, 1933.

*Man with the Calabash Pipe, The.* Boston: Houghton Mifflin, 1966.

*Mother Ditch, The.* Boston: Houghton Mifflin, 1954. Juvenile, chiefly descriptive; illustrations by Karl Larsson.

*Pause in the Desert, A.* Boston: Houghton Mifflin, 1957. Miscellany of sixteen short stories with plots drawn from crime, fantasy, western humor, Indian and school life, all but one previously published: "Old Century's River," "A Pause in the Desert," "The Touch of Greatness," "By the Boys Themselves," "Mr. Skidmore's Gift," "John the Revelator," "The Bystander," "La Spécialté de M. Duclos," "Thick on the Bay," "The Bright Faces," "To Walk in the City Streets," "Prelude to Reunion," "The Resting Place," "The Happy Indian Laughter," "The Brush of Wings," and "Spud and Cochise."

*Sparks Fly Upward.* Boston: Houghton Mifflin, 1931.

2. Nonfiction

*An Alphabet for Writing the Navajo Language* (with J. P. Harrington).
  Washington: United States Indian Service, 1936.
*As Long as the Grass Shall Grow.* New York and Toronto: Alliance Book
  Corporation, 1940.
*Changing Indian, The.* Norman: University of Oklahoma Press, 1942.
  Symposium arranged by the Association on American indian Affairs;
  edited by Oliver La Farge.
*Eagle in the Egg, The.* Boston: Houghton Mifflin, 1949.
*Introduction to American Indian Art.* New York: Exposition of Indian Tri-
  bal Arts, 1931. Part I, by John Sloan and Oliver La Farge; Part II, by
  eleven other authorities on the Indian arts and crafts.
*Pictorial History of the American Indian, A.* New York: Crown Publishers,
  1956. Issued in a rewritten edition for juveniles, with additional illus-
  trations, as *The American Indian.* New York: Golden Press, 1960.
*Raw Material.* Boston: Houghton Mifflin, 1945.
*Santa Eulalia.* Chicago: University of Chicage Press, 1947.
*Santa Fe; The Autobiography of a Southwestern Town.* With Arthur N.
  Morgan. Norman: University of Oklahoma Press, 1959.
*Tribes and Temples.* With Frans Blom. New Orleans: Tulane University
  Press, 1927.
*War Below Zero.* With Bernt Balchen and Corey Ford. Boston: Houghton
  Mifflin, 1944.
*Year Bearer's People, The.* With Douglas Byers. New Orleans: Tulane
  University Press, 1931.


3. Articles, Essays, Poems, Letters

The Oliver La Farge collection of books, manuscripts, and related materials was purchased by the University of Texas on October 20, 1965. The
collection includes a bibliography of both published and unpublished
works; first editions of all published books with outlines, typescripts, and
revisions; the manuscripts of eighty-eight short stories and seventy articles;
considerable unpublished creative and scientific material, including notebooks and linguistic data; book reviews; and published copies of the foreign
editions of German, Dutch, and Spanish translations between 1929 and
1948. *Sparks Fly Upward* was printed in Spanish in 1941, and *Cochise of
Arizona* had an Italian edition in 1956. Letters, photostats, and notes used
in connection with the preparation of this book have been placed in the
Oliver La Farge File, Coronado Room, Zimmerman Library, University
of New Mexico, Albuquerque.

*Selected Bibliography*

## SECONDARY SOURCES

1. Published Articles, Commentaries, and Reviews

ADAMS, J. DONALD. *The Shape of Books to Come.* New York: Viking, 1948. Stresses the rich mine of American folk material in the United States; names Roark Bradford, Carl Carmer, J. Frank Dobie, Mary Austin, and Oliver La Farge among the leading writers to use it.

AUSTIN, MARY. Review of *Laughing Boy. Saturday Review of Literature,* VI (November 9, 1929), 362-63. Sees the novel as more than a good story, artistically presented. Mrs. Austin believes La Farge shows interdependence in primitive marriage, as a man and woman work together for their common foothold in the wilderness.

BIRD, J. "The Future of Oliver La Farge," *Bookman,* LXXII (September, 1930), 11-14. La Farge's secret is his flair for life, his gusto. He is a poet. What he feels intensely, he talks about best.

BROOKS, VAN WYCK. *On Literature Today.* New York: Dutton, 1941. Calls the contemporary period of time one of great confusion and decries the mood of pessimism in fiction. Looks toward the regional writing centers for more positive affirmations in literature.

BUNKER, ROBERT. "Oliver La Farge: In Search of Self," *New Mexico Quarterly,* XX (Summer, 1950), 211-24. Broad range of La Farge's interests and efforts is reflected in the variety of his production. He is an anthropologist, a historian, an executive of the Association on American Indian Affairs; but in each role his primary interest remains the relationship between man and man.

DICKINSON, ASA DON. *The World's Best Books, Homer to Hemingway.* New York: H. W. Wilson, 1953. Of the five La Farge novels which Dickinson considers, he gives brief notice only to *Laughing Boy* and *Sparks Fly Upward,* identifying the first as an idyl of hapless love and the second as strife in the hero's veins between Spanish and Indian blood.

DODD, L. W. Review of *Sparks Fly Upward. Saturday Review of Literature,* VIII (November 7, 1931), 261. The novel objectively tells of living people in a three-dimensional world and is thoughtfully planned. It has substance, form, atmosphere; serenity and wisdom are implicit in its criticism of life.

FADIMAN, CLIFTON. Review of *The Copper Pot. New Yorker,* XVIII (June 20, 1942), 65. The story is balanced and perceptive, but the central character lacks intensity. The reviewer wonders whether La Farge himself may not be trying to break through a world not dissimilar to that which inhibits his hero.

FULLER, EDMUND. *Books with Men Behind Them.* New York: Random House, 1962. Compares Oliver La Farge's *Laughing Boy* with Alan

Paton's *Cry, the Beloved Country* in terms of native cultures shattered by culture of the white man. The tragedy is not that things are broken but that they are not mended again.

GASTON, EDWIN W., JR. *The Early Novel of the Southwest.* Albuquerque: University of New Mexico Press, 1961. Classifies novels about Indians according to the tribe providing the major interest.

GILLIS, EVERETT A. *Oliver La Farge.* Austin: Steck-Vaughn, 1967. La Farge wrote with ease in numerous fields—fiction, biography, professional commentary, social criticism, personal essay—and with sustained craftsmanship in every form. Paucity of invention may have led him to abandon the longer fictional form after 1942, the date of his last novel.

HATCHER, HARLAN. *Creating the Modern American Novel.* New York: Farrar and Rinehart, 1935. Credits La Farge with contributing to the revolt against the objective realism of the American novel of 1920's.

HAZLITT, HENRY. "Books in Brief." Review of *Sparks Fly Upward. Nation,* CXXXIV (January 6, 1932), 25. Characters are not emphatic enough to make the novel memorable, although the style is smooth and the revolutionary events in the plot are significant.

LAUGHLIN, RUTH A. Review of *The Enemy Gods. New Mexico Quarterly,* VIII (February, 1938), 63-64. Considers this novel a deeper, franker book than *Laughing Boy*; it faces the problem of a primitive culture encircled by an advanced civilization and tries to find an answer.

MIRRIELEES, EDITH. Review of *The Enemy Gods. Saturday Review of Literature,* XVI (October 16, 1937), 5. Both the main character and the partial portraits are of great interest. The story illuminates the history of the times, portraying not only the heartbreaking wrong of much early Indian policy but also the courageous good sense by which some parts of that wrong are being corrected.

POWELL, LAWRENCE CLARK. *Books, West and Southwest.* Los Angeles: Ward Ritchie, 1957. Compares *Laughing Boy* with Willa Cather's *Death Comes for the Archbishop* in its freedom from overstatement, overwriting, and synthetic emotions.

————. *Southwestern Book Trails.* Albuquerque: Horn and Wallace, 1963, *Behind the Mountains* may well outweigh all of the La Farge books after *Laughing Boy*.

RICKETSON, EDITH. "Oliver La Farge." *El Palacio,* LXXI-LXXII (Summer, 1964), 25. Considering his notable accomplishments in the diverse fields of science, arts, belles lettres, history, and humanitarianism, Oliver La Farge appears to have been truly a twentieth-century "Renaissance man"; but anyone who ventured to make that suggestion would have been nicked very neatly by La Farge's rapierlike wit.

ROBBINS, FRANCES LAMONT. "The Leisure Arts," *Outlook,* CLIII (November 6, 1929), 386-87. *Laughing Boy* a "glowing spot among drab novels of conventional setting and theme."

SCOTT, WINFIELD TOWNLEY. "Introduction." *The Man with the Calabash Pipe*. See La Farge, *Fiction*. La Farge remained a mixture—partly as a writer, always as a man—of East Coast and Southwest, of Groton-Harvard breeding and hard-eyed artist. Perhaps the intensity of his character throve on the conflict of his inheritance.

SIMPSON, CLINTON. Review of *Laughing Boy*. *Bookman*, LXX (January, 1930), 561. The story moves among conceptions of life so foreign to the naturalistic fiction of our day that it would seem to belong to a different kind of writing; filled with love, morals, and religion.

SPILLER, R. E. "Authentic Fictional Studies." *Literary History of the United States, A*. New York: Macmillan, 1946. Beginning with *The Delight Makers* by Adolph F. Bandelier in 1890, Hamlin Garland, Oliver La Farge, Dama M. Smith, Edwin Corle, Iola Fuller, and Charles L. McNichols have been among those who have written of the Indians with realistic insight.

STEVENS, ALDEN. "Legacy of Oliver La Farge, The." *Indian Affairs*, No. 55 (June, 1964). New York: Association on American Affairs. The successor of La Farge as president of the Association on American Indian Affairs pays tribute to his work in building and planning for its future.

THORP, WILLARD. *American Writing in the Twentieth Century*. Cambridge: Harvard University Press, 1960. Relates social emphasis in novels of the 1930's to zeal shown by Congress of Writers in 1935 and League of American Writers, which was organized in 1937 and dissolved in 1942.

"TRIBUTES." *Indian Affairs*, No. 52 (August, 1963). See STEVENS, ALDEN above. Carl Carmer, John Collier, Edna Ferber, John Hay Whitney, Adlai E. Stevenson, and others pay tribute to La Farge for his success in building a bridge of communication between the American Indians and the rest of American society.

VAN DOREN, CARL. *The American Novel, 1789-1939*. New York: Macmillan, 1946. *Laughing Boy*, the most understanding and touching study of an Indian hero since Helen Hunt Jackson's *Ramona*.

WALLACE, MARGARET. Review of *The Copper Pot*. *New York Times*, June 21, 1942, p. 7. As the grandson of John La Farge and the son of Grant La Farge, Oliver knows more than most writers about the working life of an artst; uses knowledge to portray the step-by-step progress of a gifted American painter to a painful triumph in his career.

WARFEL, HARRY R. *American Novelists of Today*. New York: American Book Company, 1951. As a writer, La Farge considers his central interest to be in the art of writing and not in any specific subject. After 1940 his literary interests shifted from Indian themes and centered upon an autobiography, short stories, a novel about the spiritual maturing of a painter in New Orleans, and a complete history of the Army Air Transport Command.

WEEKS, EDWARD. Review of *Long Pennant*. "Bookshelf." *Atlantic*, CLIII (November, 1933), 18. Mr. Weeks believes that La Farge is more at home in New England than in New Orleans. He calls the treatment of the characters in *Long Pennant* decidedly unequal but finds the novel a highly readable book.

## 2. Unpublished Critical Studies

FRIEDMAN, PHILIP. "Oliver La Farge: The Scientist as Literary Artist." M.A. thesis, University of New Mexico, 1959. La Farge helped to establish an ethnological approach toward solving the problems of Indians in the United States and concludes that the detail he emphasized as a scientist contributed to the exactitude with which he writes his literary narratives.

MC HENRY, CAROL. "Tradition: Ballast in Transition; A Literary Biography of Oliver La Farge." M.A. thesis, University of New Mexico, 1966. Traces biographical details in the writing of the author which reveal that tradition alone sustains a man in times of painful transition. Draws upon interviews with members of the writer's family; cites passages in his works.

# Index

# Index